CONSUMER PROTECTION ACT 1987 (UK)

Updated as of March 26, 2018

THE LAW LIBRARY

TABLE OF CONTENTS

Introductory Text	4
Part I Product Liability	4
Purpose and construction of Part I.	9
Power to modify Part I.	10
Application of Part I to Crown.	10
Part II Consumer Safety	11
Interpretation of Part II.	23
Part III Misleading Price Indications	25
Part IV Enforcement of Parts II and III	26
Part V Miscellaneous and Supplemental	36
Amendments of Part I of the Health and Safety at Work etc. Act 1974.	47
Schedules	48
Schedule 1. Limitation of Actions under Part I	48
Schedule 2. Prohibition Notices and Notices to Warn	52
Schedule 3. Amendments of Part I of the Health and Safety at Work etc. Act 1974	56
Schedule 4. Minor and Consequential Amendments	59
Schedule 5. Repeals	62
Open Government Licence v3.0	62

Introductory Text

Consumer Protection Act 1987

1987 CHAPTER 43

An Act to make provision with respect to the liability of persons for damage caused by defective products; to consolidate with amendments the Consumer Safety Act 1978 and the Consumer Safety (Amendment) Act 1986; to make provision with respect to the giving of price indications; to amend Part I of the Health and Safety at Work etc. Act 1974 and sections 31 and 80 of the Explosives Act 1875; to repeal the Trade Descriptions Act 1972 and the Fabrics (Misdescription) Act 1913; and for connected purposes.

[15th May 1987]

Be it enacted by the Queen's most Excellent Majesty, by and with the advice and consent of the Lords Spiritual and Temporal, and Commons, in this present Parliament assembled, and by the authority of the same, as follows:—

Extent Information

E1. Act extends to Northern Ireland with specified exceptions, see s. 49

Modifications etc. (not altering text)

C1. Act excluded (30.10.2005) by The Veterinary Medicines Regulations 2005 (S.I. 2005/2475), reg. 44

C2. By the Toys (Safety) Regulations 1989, S.I. 1989/1275, reg. 15. (1) it is provided that those Regulations shall be treated for all purposes as if they were safety regulations within the meaning of this Act

C3. Act extended (6.4.1992) by S.I. 1992/711, reg. 30

Act extended (24.2.1995) by S.I. 1995/204, reg. 16. (1)

Act applied (1.1.1995) by S.I. 1994/3142, reg. 18. (6)

C4. Act continued (1.10.2015) by The Consumer Rights Act 2015 (Commencement No. 3, Transitional Provisions, Savings and Consequential Amendments) Order 2015 (S.I. 2015/1630), art. 8. (8)

C5. Act applied in part (with modifications) (20.5.2016) by The Standardised Packaging of Tobacco Products Regulations 2015 (S.I. 2015/829), reg. 18 (with regs. 14. (5), 20)

Commencement Information

I1. Act not in force at Royal Assent see s.50; Act fully in force 1.3.1989 (subject to reservations in S.I. 1988/2076).

Part I Product Liability

Part I Product Liability

1 Purpose and construction of Part I.

(1) This Part shall have effect for the purpose of making such provision as is necessary in order to comply with the product liability Directive and shall be construed accordingly.

(2) In this Part, except in so far as the context otherwise requires—

F1...

"dependant" and "relative" have the same meaning as they have in, respectively, the M1. Fatal Accidents Act 1976 and the [F2. Damages (Scotland) Act 2011];

"producer", in relation to a product, means—

(a) the person who manufactured it;

(b) in the case of a substance which has not been manufactured but has been won or abstracted, the person who won or abstracted it;

(c) in the case of a product which has not been manufactured, won or abstracted but essential characteristics of which are attributable to an industrial or other process having been carried out (for example, in relation to agricultural produce), the person who carried out that process;

"product" means any goods or electricity and (subject to subsection (3) below) includes a product which is comprised in another product, whether by virtue of being a component part or raw material or otherwise; and

"the product liability Directive" means the Directive of the Council of the [F3. European Union], dated 25th July 1985, (No. 85/374/EEC) on the approximation of the laws, regulations and administrative provisions of the member States concerning liability for defective products.

(3) For the purposes of this Part a person who supplies any product in which products are comprised, whether by virtue of being component parts or raw materials or otherwise, shall not be treated by reason only of his supply of that product as supplying any of the products so comprised.

Amendments (Textual)

F1. Definition of "agricultural produce" in s. 1. (2) omitted (E.W.) (4.12.2000) by virtue of S.I. 2000/2771, art. 2. (2) and that same definition omitted (S.) (19.7.2001) by virtue of S.S.I. 2001/265, art. 2. (2)

F2. Words in s. 1. (2) substituted (S.) (7.7.2011) by Damages (Scotland) Act 2011 (asp 7), ss. 15, 19. (3), Sch. 1 para. 4. (1) (with ss. 17, 19. (2)); S.S.I. 2011/268, art. 3, (with art. 4)

F3. Words in s. 1. (2)(c) substituted (22.4.2011) by The Treaty of Lisbon (Changes in Terminology) Order 2011 (S.I. 2011/1043), art. 4. (1)

Marginal Citations

M1 1976 c. 30.

2 Liability for defective products.

(1) Subject to the following provisions of this Part, where any damage is caused wholly or partly by a defect in a product, every person to whom subsection (2) below applies shall be liable for the damage.

(2) This subsection applies to—

(a) the producer of the product;

(b) any person who, by putting his name on the product or using a trade mark or other distinguishing mark in relation to the product, has held himself out to be the producer of the product;

(c) any person who has imported the product into a member State from a place outside the member States in order, in the course of any business of his, to supply it to another.

(3) Subject as aforesaid, where any damage is caused wholly or partly by a defect in a product, any person who supplied the product (whether to the person who suffered the damage, to the producer of any product in which the product in question is comprised or to any other person) shall be liable for the damage if—

(a) the person who suffered the damage requests the supplier to identify one or more of the persons (whether still in existence or not) to whom subsection (2) above applies in relation to the product;

(b) that request is made within a reasonable period after the damage occurs and at a time when it is not reasonably practicable for the person making the request to identify all those persons; and

(c) the supplier fails, within a reasonable period after receiving the request, either to comply with the request or to identify the person who supplied the product to him.

F4. (4). . . . .

(5) Where two or more persons are liable by virtue of this Part for the same damage, their liability shall be joint and several.

(6) This section shall be without prejudice to any liability arising otherwise than by virtue of this Part.

Amendments (Textual)

F4. S. 2. (4) omitted (E.W.) (4.12.2000) by virtue of S.I. 2000/2771, art. 2. (3) and that same provision omitted (S.) (19.7.2001) by virtue of S.S.I. 2001/265, art. 2. (3)

Modifications etc. (not altering text)

C1. S. 2. (2)(b) amended (31.10.1994) by 1994 c. 26, s. 106. (1), Sch. 4 para. 1. (2); S.I. 1994/2550, art. 2

3 Meaning of "defect".

(1) Subject to the following provisions of this section, there is a defect in a product for the purposes of this Part if the safety of the product is not such as persons generally are entitled to expect; and for those purposes "safety", in relation to a product, shall include safety with respect to products comprised in that product and safety in the context of risks of damage to property, as well as in the context of risks of death or personal injury.

(2) In determining for the purposes of subsection (1) above what persons generally are entitled to expect in relation to a product all the circumstances shall be taken into account, including—

(a) the manner in which, and purposes for which, the product has been marketed, its get-up, the use of any mark in relation to the product and any instructions for, or warnings with respect to, doing or refraining from doing anything with or in relation to the product;

(b) what might reasonably be expected to be done with or in relation to the product; and

(c) the time when the product was supplied by its producer to another;

and nothing in this section shall require a defect to be inferred from the fact alone that the safety of a product which is supplied after that time is greater than the safety of the product in question.

4 Defences.

(1) In any civil proceedings by virtue of this Part against any person ("the person proceeded against") in respect of a defect in a product it shall be a defence for him to show—

(a) that the defect is attributable to compliance with any requirement imposed by or under any enactment or with any [F5. EU] obligation; or

(b) that the person proceeded against did not at any time supply the product to another; or

(c) that the following conditions are satisfied, that is to say—

(i) that the only supply of the product to another by the person proceeded against was otherwise than in the course of a business of that person's; and

(ii) that section 2. (2) above does not apply to that person or applies to him by virtue only of things done otherwise than with a view to profit; or

(d) that the defect did not exist in the product at the relevant time; or

(e) that the state of scientific and technical knowledge at the relevant time was not such that a producer of products of the same description as the product in question might be expected to have discovered the defect if it had existed in his products while they were under his control; or

(f) that the defect—

(i) constituted a defect in a product ("the subsequent product") in which the product in question had been comprised; and

(ii) was wholly attributable to the design of the subsequent product or to compliance by the producer of the product in question with instructions given by the producer of the subsequent product.

(2) In this section "the relevant time", in relation to electricity, means the time at which it was generated, being a time before it was transmitted or distributed, and in relation to any other product, means—

(a) if the person proceeded against is a person to whom subsection (2) of section 2 above applies in relation to the product, the time when he supplied the product to another;

(b) if that subsection does not apply to that person in relation to the product, the time when the product was last supplied by a person to whom that subsection does apply in relation to the product.

Amendments (Textual)

F5. Words in s. 4. (1)(a) substituted (22.4.2011) by The Treaty of Lisbon (Changes in Terminology) Order 2011 (S.I. 2011/1043), art. 6. (1)(e)

5 Damage giving rise to liability.

(1) Subject to the following provisions of this section, in this Part "damage" means death or personal injury or any loss of or damage to any property (including land).

(2) A person shall not be liable under section 2 above in respect of any defect in a product for the loss of or any damage to the product itself or for the loss of or any damage to the whole or any part of any product which has been supplied with the product in question comprised in it.

(3) A person shall not be liable under section 2 above for any loss of or damage to any property which, at the time it is lost or damaged, is not—

(a) of a description of property ordinarily intended for private use, occupation or consumption; and

(b) intended by the person suffering the loss or damage mainly for his own private use, occupation or consumption.

(4) No damages shall be awarded to any person by virtue of this Part in respect of any loss of or damage to any property if the amount which would fall to be so awarded to that person, apart from this subsection and any liability for interest, does not exceed £275.

(5) In determining for the purposes of this Part who has suffered any loss of or damage to property and when any such loss or damage occurred, the loss or damage shall be regarded as having occurred at the earliest time at which a person with an interest in the property had knowledge of the material facts about the loss or damage.

(6) For the purposes of subsection (5) above the material facts about any loss of or damage to any property are such facts about the loss or damage as would lead a reasonable person with an interest in the property to consider the loss or damage sufficiently serious to justify his instituting proceedings for damages against a defendant who did not dispute liability and was able to satisfy a judgment.

(7) For the purposes of subsection (5) above a person's knowledge includes knowledge which he might reasonably have been expected to acquire—

(a) from facts observable or ascertainable by him; or

(b) from facts ascertainable by him with the help of appropriate expert advice which it is reasonable for him to seek;

but a person shall not be taken by virtue of this subsection to have knowledge of a fact ascertainable by him only with the help of expert advice unless he has failed to take all reasonable steps to obtain (and, where appropriate, to act on) that advice.

(8) Subsections (5) to (7) above shall not extend to Scotland.

6 Application of certain enactments etc.

(1) Any damage for which a person is liable under section 2 above shall be deemed to have been caused—

(a) for the purposes of the M2. Fatal Accidents Act 1976, by that person's wrongful act, neglect or default;

(b) for the purposes of section 3 of the M3. Law Reform (Miscellaneous Provisions) (Scotland) Act 1940 (contribution among joint wrongdoers), by that person's wrongful act or negligent act or omission;

(c) for the purposes of [F6sections 3 to 6 of the Damages (Scotland) Act 2011](rights of relatives of a deceased), by that person's act or omission; and

(d) for the purposes of Part II of the M4. Administration of Justice Act 1982 (damages for personal injuries, etc.—Scotland), by an act or omission giving rise to liability in that person to pay damages.

(2) Where—

(a) a person's death is caused wholly or partly by a defect in a product, or a person dies after suffering damage which has been so caused;

(b) a request such as mentioned in paragraph (a) of subsection (3) of section 2 above is made to a supplier of the product by that person's personal representatives or, in the case of a person whose death is caused wholly or partly by the defect, by any dependant or relative of that person; and

(c) the conditions specified in paragraphs (b) and (c) of that subsection are satisfied in relation to that request,

this Part shall have effect for the purposes of the M5. Law Reform (Miscellaneous Provisions) Act 1934, the Fatal Accidents Act 1976 and the [F7. Damages (Scotland) Act 2011] as if liability of the supplier to that person under that subsection did not depend on that person having requested the supplier to identify certain persons or on the said conditions having been satisified in relation to a request made by that person.

(3) Section 1 of the M6. Congenital Disabilities (Civil Liability) Act 1976 shall have effect for the purposes of this Part as if—

(a) a person were answerable to a child in respect of an occurrence caused wholly or partly by a defect in a product if he is or has been liable under section 2 above in respect of any effect of the occurrence on a parent of the child, or would be so liable if the occurrence caused a parent of the child to suffer damage;

(b) the provisions of this Part relating to liability under section 2 above applied in relation to liability by virtue of paragraph (a) above under the said section 1; and

(c) subsection (6) of the said section 1 (exclusion of liability) were omitted.

(4) Where any damage is caused partly by a defect in a product and partly by the fault of the person suffering the damage, the M7. Law Reform (Contributory Negligence) Act M8 1945 and section 5 of the Fatal Accidents Act 1976 (contributory negligence) shall have effect as if the defect were the fault of every person liable by virtue of this Part for the damage caused by the defect.

(5) In subsection (4) above "fault" has the same meaning as in the said Act of 1945.

(6) Schedule 1 to this Act shall have effect for the purpose of amending the M9. Limitation Act 1980 and the M10. Prescription and Limitation (Scotland) Act 1973 in their application in relation to the bringing of actions by virtue of this Part.

(7) It is hereby declared that liability by virtue of this Part is to be treated as liability in tort for the purposes of any enactment conferring jurisdiction on any court with respect to any matter.

(8) Nothing in this Part shall prejudice the operation of section 12 of the M11. Nuclear Installations Act 1965 (rights to compensation for certain breaches of duties confined to rights under that Act).

Amendments (Textual)

F6. Words in s. 6. (1)(c) substituted (S.) (7.7.2011) by Damages (Scotland) Act 2011 (asp 7), ss. 15, 19. (3), Sch. 1 para. 4. (2)(a) (with ss. 17, 19. (2)); S.S.I. 2011/268, art. 3, (with art. 4)

F7. Words in s. 6. (2) substituted (S.) (7.7.2011) by Damages (Scotland) Act 2011 (asp 7), ss. 15,

19. (3), Sch. 1 para. 4. (2)(b) (with ss. 17, 19. (2)); S.S.I. 2011/268, art. 3, (with art. 4)
Marginal Citations
M21976 c. 30.
M31940 c. 42.
M41982 c. 53.
M51934 c. 41.
M61976 c. 28.
M71945 c. 28.
M81976 c.30.
M91980 c. 58.
M101973 c. 52.
M111965 c. 57.

7 Prohibition on exclusions from liability.

The liability of a person by virtue of this Part to a person who has suffered damage caused wholly or partly by a defect in a product, or to a dependant or relative of such a person, shall not be limited or excluded by any contract term, by any notice or by any other provision.

8 Power to modify Part I.

(1) Her Majesty may by Order in Council make such modifications of this Part and of any other enactment (including an enactment contained in the following Parts of this Act, or in an Act passed after this Act) as appear to Her Majesty in Council to be necessary or expedient in consequence of any modification of the product liability Directive which is made at any time after the passing of this Act.
(2) An Order in Council under subsection (1) above shall not be submitted to Her Majesty in Council unless a draft of the Order has been laid before, and approved by a resolution of, each House of Parliament.

9 Application of Part I to Crown.

(1) Subject to subsection (2) below, this Part shall bind the Crown.
(2) The Crown shall not, as regards the Crown's liability by virtue of this Part, be bound by this Part further than the Crown is made liable in tort or in reparation under the M12. Crown Proceedings Act 1947, as that Act has effect from time to time.
Marginal Citations
M121947 c. 44.

Purpose and construction of Part I.

1 Purpose and construction of Part I.

(1) This Part shall have effect for the purpose of making such provision as is necessary in order to comply with the product liability Directive and shall be construed accordingly.
(2) In this Part, except in so far as the context otherwise requires—
F1...
"dependant" and "relative" have the same meaning as they have in, respectively, the M1. Fatal Accidents Act 1976 and the [F2. Damages (Scotland) Act 2011];

"producer", in relation to a product, means—
   (a) the person who manufactured it;
   (b) in the case of a substance which has not been manufactured but has been won or abstracted, the person who won or abstracted it;
   (c) in the case of a product which has not been manufactured, won or abstracted but essential characteristics of which are attributable to an industrial or other process having been carried out (for example, in relation to agricultural produce), the person who carried out that process;
"product" means any goods or electricity and (subject to subsection (3) below) includes a product which is comprised in another product, whether by virtue of being a component part or raw material or otherwise; and
"the product liability Directive" means the Directive of the Council of the [F3. European Union], dated 25th July 1985, (No. 85/374/EEC) on the approximation of the laws, regulations and administrative provisions of the member States concerning liability for defective products.
(3) For the purposes of this Part a person who supplies any product in which products are comprised, whether by virtue of being component parts or raw materials or otherwise, shall not be treated by reason only of his supply of that product as supplying any of the products so comprised.

Amendments (Textual)
F1. Definition of "agricultural produce" in s. 1. (2) omitted (E.W.) (4.12.2000) by virtue of S.I. 2000/2771, art. 2. (2) and that same definition omitted (S.) (19.7.2001) by virtue of S.S.I. 2001/265, art. 2. (2)
F2. Words in s. 1. (2) substituted (S.) (7.7.2011) by Damages (Scotland) Act 2011 (asp 7), ss. 15, 19. (3), Sch. 1 para. 4. (1) (with ss. 17, 19. (2)); S.S.I. 2011/268, art. 3, (with art. 4)
F3. Words in s. 1. (2)(c) substituted (22.4.2011) by The Treaty of Lisbon (Changes in Terminology) Order 2011 (S.I. 2011/1043), art. 4. (1)

Marginal Citations
M11976 c. 30.

Power to modify Part I.

8 Power to modify Part I.

(1) Her Majesty may by Order in Council make such modifications of this Part and of any other enactment (including an enactment contained in the following Parts of this Act, or in an Act passed after this Act) as appear to Her Majesty in Council to be necessary or expedient in consequence of any modification of the product liability Directive which is made at any time after the passing of this Act.
(2) An Order in Council under subsection (1) above shall not be submitted to Her Majesty in Council unless a draft of the Order has been laid before, and approved by a resolution of, each House of Parliament.

Application of Part I to Crown.

9 Application of Part I to Crown.

(1) Subject to subsection (2) below, this Part shall bind the Crown.
(2) The Crown shall not, as regards the Crown's liability by virtue of this Part, be bound by this Part further than the Crown is made liable in tort or in reparation under the M1. Crown Proceedings Act 1947, as that Act has effect from time to time.

Marginal Citations
M11947 c. 44.

Part II Consumer Safety

Part II Consumer Safety

Modifications etc. (not altering text)
C1. Part II : definition of "supply" applied (E.W.)(1.12.1991) by Statutory Water Companies Act 1991 (c. 58, SIF 130), ss. 1. (6), 17. (2)
C2. Pt. II applied in part (with modifications) (20.5.2016) by The Tobacco and Related Products Regulations 2016 (S.I. 2016/507), regs. 1. (2), 53. (3)

10 The general safety requirement.

F1. . . . .
Amendments (Textual)
F1. S. 10 omitted (1.10.2005) by virtue of The General Product Safety Regulations 2005 (S.I. 2005/1803, reg. 46. (2) (with regs. 42, 43)

11 Safety regulations.

(1) The Secretary of State may by regulations under this section ("safety regulations") make such provision as he considers appropriate F2. . . for the purpose of securing—
  (a) that goods to which this section applies are safe;
  (b) that goods to which this section applies which are unsafe, or would be unsafe in the hands of persons of a particular description, are not made available to persons generally or, as the case may be, to persons of that description; and
  (c) that appropriate information is, and inappropriate information is not, provided in relation to goods to which this section applies.
(2) Without prejudice to the generality of subsection (1) above, safety regulations may contain provision—
  (a) with respect to the composition or contents, design, construction, finish or packing of goods to which this section applies, with respect to standards for such goods and with respect to other matters relating to such goods;
  (b) with respect to the giving, refusal, alteration or cancellation of approvals of such goods, of descriptions of such goods or of standards for such goods;
  (c) with respect to the conditions that may be attached to any approval given under the regulations;
  (d) for requiring such fees as may be determined by or under the regulations to be paid on the giving or alteration of any approval under the regulations and on the making of an application for such an approval or alteration;
  (e) with respect to appeals against refusals, alterations and cancellations of approvals given under the regulations and against the conditions contained in such approvals;
  (f) for requiring goods to which this section applies to be approved under the regulations or to conform to the requirements of the regulations or to descriptions or standards specified in or approved by or under the regulations;
  (g) with respect to the testing or inspection of goods to which this section applies (including provision for determining the standards to be applied in carrying out any test or inspection);
  (h) with respect to the ways of dealing with goods of which some or all do not satisfy a test

required by or under the regulations or a standard connected with a procedure so required;

(i) for requiring a mark, warning or instruction or any other information relating to goods to be put on or to accompany the goods or to be used or provided in some other manner in relation to the goods, and for securing that inappropriate information is not given in relation to goods either by means of misleading marks or otherwise;

(j) for prohibiting persons from supplying, or from offering to supply, agreeing to supply, exposing for supply or possessing for supply, goods to which this section applies and component parts and raw materials for such goods;

(k) for requiring information to be given to any such person as may be determined by or under the regulations for the purpose of enabling that person to exercise any function conferred on him by the regulations.

(3) Without prejudice as aforesaid, safety regulations may contain provision—

(a) for requiring persons on whom functions are conferred by or under section 27 below to have regard, in exercising their functions so far as relating to any provision of safety regulations, to matters specified in a direction issued by the Secretary of State with respect to that provision;

(b) for securing that a person shall not be guilty of an offence under section 12 below unless it is shown that the goods in question do not conform to a particular standard;

(c) for securing that proceedings for such an offence are not brought in England and Wales except by or with the consent of the Secretary of State or the Director of Public Prosecutions;

(d) for securing that proceedings for such an offence are not brought in Northern Ireland except by or with the consent of the Secretary of State or the Director of Public Prosecutions for Northern Ireland;

(e) for enabling a magistrates' court in England and Wales or Northern Ireland to try an information or, in Northern Ireland, a complaint in respect of such an offence if the information was laid or the complaint made within twelve months from the time when the offence was committed;

(f) for enabling summary proceedings for such an offence to be brought in Scotland at any time within twelve months from the time when the offence was committed; and

(g) for determining the persons by whom, and the manner in which, anything required to be done by or under the regulations is to be done.

(4) Safety regulations shall not provide for any contravention of the regulations to be an offence.

(5) Where the Secretary of State proposes to make safety regulations it shall be his duty before he makes them—

(a) to consult such organisations as appear to him to be representative of interests substantially affected by the proposal;

(b) to consult such other persons as he considers appropriate; and

(c) in the case of proposed regulations relating to goods suitable for use at work, to consult [F3the Health and Safety Executive] in relation to the application of the proposed regulations to Great Britain;

but the preceding provisions of this subsection shall not apply in the case of regulations which provide for the regulations to cease to have effect at the end of a period of not more than twelve months beginning with the day on which they come into force and which contain a statement that it appears to the Secretary of State that the need to protect the public requires that the regulations should be made without delay.

(6) The power to make safety regulations shall be exercisable by statutory instrument subject to annulment in pursuance of a resolution of either House of Parliament and shall include power—

(a) to make different provision for different cases; and

(b) to make such supplemental, consequential and transitional provision as the Secretary of State considers appropriate.

(7) This section applies to any goods other than—

(a) growing crops and things comprised in land by virtue of being attached to it;

(b) water, food, feeding stuff and fertiliser;

(c) gas which is, is to be or has been supplied by a person authorised to supply it by or under

[F4section 7. A of the Gas Act 1986 (licensing of gas suppliers and gas shippers) or paragraph 5 of Schedule 2. A to that Act (supply to very large customers an exception to prohibition on unlicensed activities)][F5or under Article 8. (1)(c) of the Gas (Northern Ireland) Order 1996];

(d) controlled drugs and licensed medicinal products.

Subordinate Legislation Made

P1. S. 11: power conferred by s. 11 exercised by S.I. 1991/1530

S. 11: s. 11 power exercised (28. 11. 1991) by S.I. 1991/2693.

P2. S. 11. (5) power exercised by S.I. 1991/447.

P3. S. 11. (5) power previously exercised by S.I. 1989/2358, 2347, 2288, 2233, 1291, 1275, 1988/1647, 1324, 1979, 1911.

Amendments (Textual)

F2. Words in s. 11. (1) omitted (1.10.2005) by virtue of The General Product Safety Regulations 2005 (S.I. 2005/1803), reg. 46. (3) (with regs. 42, 43)

F3. Words in s. 11. (5)(c) substituted (1.4.2008) by The Legislative Reform (Health and Safety Executive) Order 2008 (S.I. 2008/960), art. 22, Sch. 3 (with art. 21, Sch. 2)

F4. Words in s. 11. (7)(c) substituted (E.W.S.) (1.3.1996) by 1995 c. 45, s. 16. (1), Sch. 4 para. 15. (2); S.I. 1996/218, art. 2

F5. Words in s. 11. (7)(c) inserted (N.I.) (10.6.1996) by S.I. 1996/276 (N.I. 2), art. 71. (1), Sch. 6 (with Sch. 7 paras. 2, 3. (2)); S.R. 1996/216, art. 2

Modifications etc. (not altering text)

C2. Pt. II applied in part (with modifications) (20.5.2016) by The Tobacco and Related Products Regulations 2016 (S.I. 2016/507), regs. 1. (2), 53. (3)

C3. S. 11 applied (N.I.) (1.12.1993) by S.R. 1993/412, reg. 19. (3)

C4. S. 11. (3)(c)(e)(f) applied (with modifications) (E.W.S.) (28.11.2003 for certain purposes, 15.7.2004 for certain further purposes and otherwise prosp.) by Fireworks Act 2003 (c. 22), ss. 11. (6), 18 (with s. 2. (8)); S.I. 2003/3084, art. 2, Sch.; S.I. 2004/1831, art. 2, Sch.

C5. S. 11. (3)(f): certain functions made exercisable concurrently (29.7.2004) by The Scotland Act 1998 (Transfer of Functions to the Scottish Ministers etc.) Order 2004 (S.I. 2004/2030), art. 4, Sch.

C6. S. 11. (5) excluded (1.8.2002) by S.I. 2002/1770, reg. 1. (2)

12 Offences against the safety regulations.

(1) Where safety regulations prohibit a person from supplying or offering or agreeing to supply any goods or from exposing or possessing any goods for supply, that person shall be guilty of an offence if he contravenes the prohibition.

(2) Where safety regulations require a person who makes or processes any goods in the course of carrying on a business—

(a) to carry out a particular test or use a particular procedure in connection with the making or processing of the goods with a view to ascertaining whether the goods satisfy any requirements of such regulations; or

(b) to deal or not to deal in a particular way with a quantity of the goods of which the whole or part does not satisfy such a test or does not satisfy standards connected with such a procedure, that person shall be guilty of an offence if he does not comply with the requirement.

(3) If a person contravenes a provision of safety regulations which prohibits or requires the provision, by means of a mark or otherwise, of information of a particular kind in relation to goods, he shall be guilty of an offence.

(4) Where safety regulations require any person to give information to another for the purpose of enabling that other to exercise any function, that person shall be guilty of an offence if—

(a) he fails without reasonable cause to comply with the requirement; or

(b) in giving the information which is required of him—

(i) he makes any statement which he knows is false in a material particular; or

(ii) he recklessly makes any statement which is false in a material particular.

(5) A person guilty of an offence under this section shall be liable on summary conviction to imprisonment for a term not exceeding sixmonths or to a fine not exceeding level 5 on the standard scale or to both.

Modifications etc. (not altering text)

C7. S. 12 applied (N.I.)(1.12.1993) by S.R. 1993/412, reg. 19. (3)

S. 12 applied (1.9.1993) by S.I. 1993/1746, reg. 18. (3)

S. 12 applied (31.1.1995) by S.I. 1994/3247, art. 16. (3)

C8. S. 12 applied (with mofifications) (N.I.) (1.6.2015) by The Biocidal Products and Chemicals (Appointment of Authorities and Enforcement) Regulations (Northern Ireland) 2013 (S.R. 2013/206), regs. 2. (2), 17. (5) (with regs. 3, 19)

C9. S. 12 applied (with modifications) (E.W.S.) (1.6.2015) by The Biocidal Products and Chemicals (Appointment of Authorities and Enforcement) Regulations 2013 (S.I. 2013/1506), regs. 2. (2), 18. (5) (with reg. 3. (4)(5)31)

C10. S. 12. (5) excluded (29.4.2010) by The Aerosol Dispensers Regulations 2009 (S.I. 2009/2824), reg. 6. (3)

13 Prohibition notices and notices to warn.

(1) The Secretary of State may—

(a) serve on any person a notice ("a prohibition notice") prohibiting that person, except with the consent of the Secretary of State, from supplying, or from offering to supply, agreeing to supply, exposing for supply or possessing for supply, any relevant goods which the Secretary of State considers are unsafe and which are described in the notice;

(b) serve on any person a notice ("a notice to warn") requiring that person at his own expense to publish, in a form and manner and on occasions specified in the notice, a warning about any relevant goods which the Secretary of State considers are unsafe, which that person supplies or has supplied and which are described in the notice.

(2) Schedule 2 to this Act shall have effect with respect to prohibition notices and notices to warn; and the Secretary of State may by regulations make provision specifying the manner in which information is to be given to any person under that Schedule.

(3) A consent given by the Secretary of State for the purposes of a prohibition notice may impose such conditions on the doing of anything for which the consent is required as the Secretary of State considers appropriate.

(4) A person who contravenes a prohibition notice or a notice to warn shall be guilty of an offence and liable on summary conviction to imprisonment for a term not exceeding [F6three months] or to a fine not exceeding level 5 on the standard scale or to both.

(5) The power to make regulations under subsection (2) above shall be exercisable by statutory instrument subject to annulment in pursuance of a resolution of either House of Parliament and shall include power—

(a) to make different provision for different cases; and

(b) to make such supplemental, consequential and transitional provision as the Secretary of State considers appropriate.

(6) In this section "relevant goods" means—

(a) in relation to a prohibition notice, any goods to which section 11 above applies; and

(b) in relation to a notice to warn, any goods to which that section applies or any growing crops or things comprised in land by virtue of being attached to it.

[F7. (7)A notice may not be given under this section in respect of any aspect of the safety of goods, or any risk or category of risk associated with goods, concerning which provision is contained in the General Product Safety Regulations 2005.]

Amendments (Textual)

F6. Words in s. 13. (4) substituted (3.10.1994) by S.I. 1994/2328, reg. 11. (d) (which said S.I.

1994/2328 was revoked (1.10.2005) by S.I. 2005/1803, reg. 1. (2),
F7. S. 13. (7) inserted (1.10.2005) by The General Product Safety Regulations 2005 (S.I. 2005/1803), reg. 46. (4) (with regs. 42, 43)
Modifications etc. (not altering text)
C2. Pt. II applied in part (with modifications) (20.5.2016) by The Tobacco and Related Products Regulations 2016 (S.I. 2016/507), regs. 1. (2), 53. (3)
C11. S. 13 applied (1.1.1993) by S.I. 1992/3139, reg. 3. (2)(a) (which said S.I. 1992/3139 was revoked (15.5.2002) by S.I. 2002/1144, reg. 1. (2), Sch. 11 para. 1)
S. 13 applied (3.10.1994) by S.I. 1994/2328, reg. 11. (a)
S. 13 restricted (1.1.1995 until end of 1996) by S.I. 1994/2326, reg. 5
S. 13 restricted (24.2.1995) by S.I. 1995/204, reg. 10. (11)
S. 13 applied (with modifications) (9.1.1995) by S.I. 1994/3260, reg. 13. (1)
S. 13 applied (with modifications) (29.11.1999) by S.I. 1999/2001, reg. 24, Sch. 8 para. 2. (b)
S. 13 extended (7.6.2000) by S.I. 2000/1315, reg. 18. (6)
S. 13 applied (with modifications) (15.5.2002) by S.I. 2002/1144, regs. 2. (2), 16. (1)-(3), Sch. 10 paras. 1, 3
C12. S. 13 applied (with modifications) (17.8.2015) by The Pyrotechnic Articles (Safety) Regulations 2015 (S.I. 2015/1553), reg. 1, Sch. 7 paras. 1. (a), 2
C13. S. 13 applied (with modifications) (8.12.2016) by The Lifts Regulations 2016 (S.I. 2016/1093), reg. 1, Sch. 7 paras. 1. (a), 2 (with regs. 3-5)
C14. S. 13 applied (with modifications) (8.12.2016) by The Pressure Equipment (Safety) Regulations 2016 (S.I. 2016/1105), reg. 1, Sch. 7 paras. 1. (a), 2 (with reg. 88)
C15. S. 13 applied (with modifications) (8.12.2016) by The Electromagnetic Compatibility Regulations 2016 (S.I. 2016/1091), reg. 1, Sch. 7 paras. 1, 2 (with regs. 74, 75. (5))
C16. S. 13 applied (with modifications) (8.12.2016) by The Electrical Equipment (Safety) Regulations 2016 (S.I. 2016/1101), reg. 1, Sch. 3 paras. 1, 2 (with reg. 3)
C17. S. 13 applied (with modifications) (8.12.2016) by The Simple Pressure Vessels (Safety) Regulations 2016 (S.I. 2016/1092), reg. 1, Sch. 5 paras. 1. (a), 2 (with reg. 3)
C18. S. 13 applied (with modifications) (3.8.2017) by The Recreational Craft Regulations 2017 (S.I. 2017/737), reg. 1, Sch. 13 paras. 1. (a), 2 (with reg. 89)
C19. S. 13 applied (with modifications) (26.12.2017) by The Radio Equipment Regulations 2017 (S.I. 2017/1206), reg. 1, Sch. 10 paras. 1, 2 (with regs. 3-5, 77)

14 Suspension notices.

(1) Where an enforcement authority has reasonable grounds for suspecting that any safety provision has been contravened in relation to any goods, the authority may serve a notice ("a suspension notice") prohibiting the person on whom it is served, for such period ending not more than six months after the date of the notice as is specified therein, from doing any of the following things without the consent of the authority, that is to say, supplying the goods, offering to supply them, agreeing to supply them or exposing them for supply.

(2) A suspension notice served by an enforcement authority in respect of any goods shall—
   (a) describe the goods in a manner sufficient to identify them;
   (b) set out the grounds on which the authority suspects that a safety provision has been contravened in relation to the goods; and
   (c) state that, and the manner in which, the person on whom the notice is served may appeal against the notice under section 15 below.

(3) A suspension notice served by an enforcement authority for the purpose of prohibiting a person for any period from doing the things mentioned in subsection (1) above in relation to any goods may also require that person to keep the authority informed of the whereabouts throughout that period of any of those goods in which he has an interest.

(4) Where a suspension notice has been served on any person in respect of any goods, no further

such notice shall be served on that person in respect of the same goods unless—
  (a) proceedings against that person for an offence in respect of a contravention in relation to the goods of a safety provision (not being an offence under this section); or
  (b) proceedings for the forfeiture of the goods under section 16 or 17 below,
are pending at the end of the period specified in the first-mentioned notice.
(5) A consent given by an enforcement authority for the purposes of subsection (1) above may impose such conditions on the doing of anything for which the consent is required as the authority considers appropriate.
(6) Any person who contravenes a suspension notice shall be guilty of an offence and liable on summary conviction to imprisonment for a term not exceeding [F8three months] or to a fine not exceeding level 5 on the standard scale or to both.
(7) Where an enforcement authority serves a suspension notice in respect of any goods, the authority shall be liable to pay compensation to any person having an interest in the goods in respect of any loss or damage caused by reason of the service of the notice if—
  (a) there has been no contravention in relation to the goods of any safety provision; and
  (b) the exercise of the power is not attributable to any neglect or default by that person.
(8) Any disputed question as to the right to or the amount of any compensation payable under this section shall be determined by arbitration or, in Scotland, by a single arbiter appointed, failing agreement between the parties, by the sheriff.

Amendments (Textual)
F8. Words in s. 14. (6) substituted (3.10.1994) by S.I. 1994/2328, reg. 11. (d)

Modifications etc. (not altering text)
C2. Pt. II applied in part (with modifications) (20.5.2016) by The Tobacco and Related Products Regulations 2016 (S.I. 2016/507), regs. 1. (2), 53. (3)
C20. S. 14 applied (with modifications) (1.1.1993) by S.I. 1992/3073, reg. 28, Sch. 6 para. 3. (c)
Ss. 14-18 amended (3.10.1994) by S.I. 1994/2328, reg. 11. (b)
S. 14 excluded (1.1.1995) by S.I. 1994/2326, reg. 4. (1) (which said S.I. 2002/2326 was revoked (15.5.2002) by S.I. 2002/1144, reg. 1. (2), Sch. 11 para. 3)
S. 14 restricted (1.1.1995 until end of 1996) by S.I. 1994/2326, reg. 5
S. 14 restricted (24.2.1995) by S.I. 1995/204, reg. 10. (11)
S. 14 applied (with modifications) (9.1.1995) by S.I. 1994/3260, reg. 13. (1)
S. 14 applied (with modifications) (1.7.1997) by S.I. 1997/831, reg. 19. (1)-(4), Sch. 15 para. 2. (b) (with Sch. 15 para. 7) S. 14 applied (with modifications) (31.5.1998) by S.I. 1998/1165, reg. 13. (2)(a) (which said S.I. was revoked (25.8.2003) by S.I. 2003/1941, reg. 1. (2))
S. 14 applied (with modifications) (26.4.1999) by S.I. 1999/1053, reg. 16. (3)(a)
S. 14 applied (with modifications) (29.11.1999) by S.I. 1999/2001, reg. 24, Sch. 8 para. 2. (c)
S. 14 applied (with modifications) (8.4.2000) by S.I. 2000/730, reg. 18. (1), Sch. 9 para. 1. (2)
S. 14 excluded (7.6.2000) by S.I. 2000/1315, reg. 19. (2)
S. 14 restricted (13.6.2002) by S.I. 2002/618, reg. 62
S. 14 modified (13.6.2002) by S.I. 2002/618, reg. 63
S. 14 applied (with modifications) (15.5.2002) by S.I. 2002/1144, regs. 2. (2), 16. (1)-(3), Sch. 10 paras. 1, 3
S. 14 applied (with modifications) (25.8.2003) by S.I. 2003/1941, reg. 8, Sch. IV para. 2. (a)
C21. S. 14 applied (with modifications) (17.8.2015) by The Pyrotechnic Articles (Safety) Regulations 2015 (S.I. 2015/1553), reg. 1, Sch. 7 paras. 1. (b), 2
C22. S. 14 applied (with modifications) (1.10.2015) by The Packaging (Essential Requirements) Regulations 2015 (S.I. 2015/1640), reg. 1, Sch. 4 para. 1. (1)(a) (with reg. 3. (5))
C23. S. 14 applied (with modifications) (8.12.2016) by The Simple Pressure Vessels (Safety) Regulations 2016 (S.I. 2016/1092), reg. 1, Sch. 5 paras. 1. (b), 2 (with reg. 3)
C24. S. 14 applied (with modifications) (8.12.2016) by The Electrical Equipment (Safety) Regulations 2016 (S.I. 2016/1101), reg. 1, Sch. 3 paras. 1, 2 (with reg. 3)
C25. S. 14 applied (with modifications) (8.12.2016) by The Electromagnetic Compatibility Regulations 2016 (S.I. 2016/1091), reg. 1, Sch. 7 paras. 1, 2 (with regs. 74, 75. (5))

C26. S. 14 applied (with modifications) (8.12.2016) by The Pressure Equipment (Safety) Regulations 2016 (S.I. 2016/1105), reg. 1, Sch. 7 paras. 1. (b), 2 (with reg. 88)
C27. S. 14 applied (with modifications) (8.12.2016) by The Lifts Regulations 2016 (S.I. 2016/1093), reg. 1, Sch. 7 paras. 1. (b), 2 (with regs. 3-5)
C28. S. 14 applied (with modifications) (3.8.2017) by The Recreational Craft Regulations 2017 (S.I. 2017/737), reg. 1, Sch. 13 paras. 1. (b), 2 (with reg. 89)
C29. S. 14 applied (with modifications) (26.12.2017) by The Radio Equipment Regulations 2017 (S.I. 2017/1206), reg. 1, Sch. 10 paras. 1, 2 (with regs. 3-5, 77)
C30. S. 14. (6) modified (20.5.2016) by The Tobacco and Related Products Regulations 2016 (S.I. 2016/507), regs. 1. (2), 53. (4)

15 Appeals against suspension notices.

(1) Any person having an interest in any goods in respect of which a suspension notice is for the time being in force may apply for an order setting aside the notice.
(2) An application under this section may be made—
   (a) to any magistrates' court in which proceedings have been brought in England and Wales or Northern Ireland—
(i) for an offence in respect of a contravention in relation to the goods of any safety provision; or
(ii) for the forfeiture of the goods under section 16 below;
   (b) where no such proceedings have been so brought, by way of complaint to a magistrates' court; or
   (c) in Scotland, by summary application to the sheriff.
(3) On an application under this section to a magistrates' court in England and Wales or Northern Ireland the court shall make an order setting aside the suspension notice only if the court is satisfied that there has been no contravention in relation to the goods of any safety provision.
(4) On an application under this section to the sheriff he shall make an order setting aside the suspension notice only if he is satisfied that at the date of making the order—
   (a) proceedings for an offence in respect of a contravention in relation to the goods of any safety provision; or
   (b) proceedings for the forfeiture of the goods under section 17 below,
have not been brought or, having been brought, have been concluded.
(5) Any person aggrieved by an order made under this section by a magistrates' court in England and Wales or Northern Ireland, or by a decision of such a court not to make such an order, may appeal against that order or decision—
   (a) in England and Wales, to the Crown Court;
   (b) in Northern Ireland, to the county court;
and an order so made may contain such provision as appears to the court to be appropriate for delaying the coming into force of the order pending the making and determination of any appeal (including any application under section 111 of the M1. Magistrates' Courts Act 1980 or Article 146 of the M2. Magistrates' Courts (Northern Ireland) Order 1981 (statement of case)).
Modifications etc. (not altering text)
C2. Pt. II applied in part (with modifications) (20.5.2016) by The Tobacco and Related Products Regulations 2016 (S.I. 2016/507), regs. 1. (2), 53. (3)
C31. S. 15 applied (with modifications) (1.1.1993) by S.I. 1992/3073, reg. 28, Sch. 6 para. 3. (c).
Ss. 14-18 amended (3.10.1994) by S.I. 1994/2328, reg. 11. (b)
S. 15 applied (with modifications) (1.7.1997) by S.I. 1997/831, reg. 19. (1)-(4), Sch. 15 para. 2. (b) (with Sch. 15 para. 7)
S. 15 applied (with modifications) (31.5.1998) by S.I. 1998/1165, reg. 13. (2)(a) (which said S.I. was revoked (25.8.2003) by S.I. 2003/1941, reg. 1. (2))
S. 15 applied (with modifications) (26.4.1999) by S.I. 1999/1053, reg. 16. (3)(a)
S. 15 applied (with modifications) (29.11.1999) by S.I. 1999/2001, reg. 24, Sch. 8 para. 2. (c)

S. 15 applied (with modifications) (8.4.2000) by S.I. 2000/730, reg. 18. (1), Sch. 9 para. 1. (2)
S. 15 modified (13.6.2002) by S.I. 2002/618, reg. 63
S. 15 applied (with modifications) (15.5.2002) by S.I. 2002/1144, regs. 2. (2), 16. (1)-(3), Sch. 10 paras. 1, 3
S. 15 applied (with modifications) (25.8.2003) by S.I. 2003/1941, reg. 8, Sch. IV para. 2. (a)
C32. S. 15 applied (with modifications) (1.10.2015) by The Packaging (Essential Requirements) Regulations 2015 (S.I. 2015/1640), reg. 1, Sch. 4 para. 1. (1)(a) (with reg. 3. (5))
Marginal Citations
M1 1980 c.43.
M2. S.I. 1981/1675 (N.I. 26).

16 Forfeiture: England and Wales and Northern Ireland.

(1) An enforcement authority in England and Wales or Northern Ireland may apply under this section for an order for the forfeiture of any goods on the grounds that there has been a contravention in relation to the goods of a safety provision.

(2) An application under this section may be made—

(a) where proceedings have been brought in a magistrates' court for an offence in respect of a contravention in relation to some or all of the goods of any safety provision, to that court;

(b) where an application with respect to some or all of the goods has been made to a magistrates' court under section 15 above or section 33 below, to that court; and

(c) where no application for the forfeiture of the goods has been made under paragraph (a) or (b) above, by way of complaint to a magistrates' court.

(3) On an application under this section the court shall make an order for the forfeiture of any goods only if it is satisfied that there has been a contravention in relation to the goods of a safety provision.

(4) For the avoidance of doubt it is declared that a court may infer for the purposes of this section that there has been a contravention in relation to any goods of a safety provision if it is satisfied that any such provision has been contravened in relation to goods which are representative of those goods (whether by reason of being of the same design or part of the same consignment or batch or otherwise).

(5) Any person aggrieved by an order made under this section by a magistrates' court, or by a decision of such a court not to make such an order, may appeal against that order or decision—

(a) in England and Wales, to the Crown Court;

(b) in Northern Ireland, to the county court;

and an order so made may contain such provision as appears to the court to be appropriate for delaying the coming into force of the order pending the making and determination of any appeal (including any application under section 111 of the Magistrates' Courts Act 1980 or Article 146 of the Magistrates' Courts (Northern Ireland) Order 1981 (statement of case)).

(6) Subject to subsection (7) below, where any goods are forfeited under this section they shall be destroyed in accordance with such directions as the court may give.

(7) On making an order under this section a magistrates' court may, if it considers it appropriate to do so, direct that the goods to which the order relates shall (instead of being destroyed) be released, to such person as the court may specify, on condition that that person—

(a) does not supply those goods to any person otherwise than as mentioned in section 46. (7)(a) or (b) below; and

(b) complies with any order to pay costs or expenses (including any order under section 35 below) which has been made against that person in the proceedings for the order for forfeiture.

Modifications etc. (not altering text)
C2. Pt. II applied in part (with modifications) (20.5.2016) by The Tobacco and Related Products Regulations 2016 (S.I. 2016/507), regs. 1. (2), 53. (3)
C33. Ss. 14-18 amended (3.10.1994) by S.I. 1994/2328, reg. 11. (b)

S. 16 excluded (1.1.1995) by S.I. 1994/2326, reg. 4. (1) (which said S.I. 1994/2326 was revoked (15.5.2002) by S.I. 2002/1144, reg. 1. (2), Sch. 11 para. 3)
S. 16 restricted (1.1.1995 until end of 1996) by S.I. 1996/2326, reg. 5
S. 16 restricted (24.2.1995) by S.I. 1995/204, reg. 10. (11)
S. 16 applied (with modifications) (9.1.1995) by S.I. 1994/3260, reg. 13. (1)
S. 16 excluded (7.6.2000) by S.I. 2000/1315, reg. 19. (2)
S. 16 restricted (13.6.2002) by S.I. 2002/618, reg. 62
S. 16 modified (13.6.2002) by S.I. 2002/618, reg. 63
S. 16 applied (with modifications) (15.5.2002) by S.I. 2002/1144, regs. 2. (2), 16. (1)-(3), Sch. 10 paras. 1, 3
C34. S. 16 applied (with modifications) (17.8.2015) by The Pyrotechnic Articles (Safety) Regulations 2015 (S.I. 2015/1553), reg. 1, Sch. 7 paras. 1. (c), 2
C35. S. 16 applied (with modifications) (8.12.2016) by The Electromagnetic Compatibility Regulations 2016 (S.I. 2016/1091), reg. 1, Sch. 7 paras. 1, 2 (with regs. 74, 75. (5))
C36. S. 16 applied (with modifications) (8.12.2016) by The Pressure Equipment (Safety) Regulations 2016 (S.I. 2016/1105), reg. 1, Sch. 7 paras. 1. (c), 2 (with reg. 88)
C37. S. 16 applied (with modifications) (8.12.2016) by The Simple Pressure Vessels (Safety) Regulations 2016 (S.I. 2016/1092), reg. 1, Sch. 5 paras. 1. (c), 2 (with reg. 3)
C38. S. 16 applied (with modifications) (8.12.2016) by The Electrical Equipment (Safety) Regulations 2016 (S.I. 2016/1101), reg. 1, Sch. 3 paras. 1, 2 (with reg. 3)
C39. S. 16 applied (with modifications) (8.12.2016) by The Lifts Regulations 2016 (S.I. 2016/1093), reg. 1, Sch. 7 paras. 1. (c), 2 (with regs. 3-5)
C40. S. 16 applied (with modifications) (3.8.2017) by The Recreational Craft Regulations 2017 (S.I. 2017/737), reg. 1, Sch. 13 paras. 1. (c), 2 (with reg. 89)
C41. S. 16 applied (with modifications) (26.12.2017) by The Radio Equipment Regulations 2017 (S.I. 2017/1206), reg. 1, Sch. 10 paras. 1, 2 (with regs. 3-5, 77)

17 Forfeiture: Scotland.

(1) In Scotland a sheriff may make an order for forfeiture of any goods in relation to which there has been a contravention of a safety provision—
   (a) on an application by the procurator-fiscal made in the manner specified in section 310 of the M3. Criminal Procedure (Scotland) Act 1975; or
   (b) where a person is convicted of any offence in respect of any such contravention, in addition to any other penalty which the sheriff may impose.
(2) The procurator-fiscal making an application under subsection (1)(a) above shall serve on any person appearing to him to be the owner of, or otherwise to have an interest in, the goods to which the application relates a copy of the application, together with a notice giving him the opportunity to appear at the hearing of the application to show cause why the goods should not be forfeited.
(3) Service under subsection (2) above shall be carried out, and such service may be proved, in the manner specified for citation of an accused in summary proceedings under the Criminal Procedure (Scotland) Act 1975.
(4) Any person upon whom notice is served under subsection (2) above and any other person claiming to be the owner of, or otherwise to have an interest in, goods to which an application under this section relates shall be entitled to appear at the hearing of the application to show cause why the goods should not be forfeited.
(5) The sheriff shall not make an order following an application under subsection (1)(a) above—
   (a) if any person on whom notice is served under subsection (2) above does not appear, unless service of the notice on that person is proved; or
   (b) if no notice under subsection (2) above has been served, unless the court is satisfied that in the circumstances it was reasonable not to serve notice on any person.
(6) The sheriff shall make an order under this section only if he is satisfied that there has been a

contravention in relation to those goods of a safety provision.

(7) For the avoidance of doubt it is declared that the sheriff may infer for the purposes of this section that there has been a contravention in relation to any goods of a safety provision if he is satisfied that any such provision has been contravened in relation to any goods which are representative of those goods (whether by reason of being of the same design or part of the same consignment or batch or otherwise).

(8) Where an order for the forfeiture of any goods is made following an application by the procurator-fiscal under subsection (1)(a) above, any person who appeared, or was entitled to appear, to show cause why goods should not be forfeited may, within twenty-one days of the making of the order, appeal to the High Court by Bill of Suspension on the ground of an alleged miscarriage of justice; [F9and section 182. (5)(a) to (e) of the Criminal Procedure (Scotland) Act 1995 shall apply to an appeal under this subsection as it applies to a stated case under Part X of that Act].

(9) An order following an application under subsection (1)(a) above shall not take effect—

(a) until the end of the period of twenty-one days beginning with the day after the day on which the order is made; or

(b) if an appeal is made under subsection (8) above within that period, until the appeal is determined or abandoned.

(10) An order under subsection (1)(b) above shall not take effect—

(a) until the end of the period within which an appeal against the order could be brought under the Criminal Procedure (Scotland) Act 1975; or

(b) if an appeal is made within that period, until the appeal is determined or abandoned.

(11) Subject to subsection (12) below, goods forfeited under this section shall be destroyed in accordance with such directions as the sheriff may give.

(12) If he thinks fit, the sheriff may direct that the goods be released, to such person as he may specify, on condition that that person does not supply those goods to any other person otherwise than as mentioned in section 46. (7)(a) or (b) below.

Amendments (Textual)

F9. Words in s. 17. (8) substituted (1.4.1996) by 1995 c. 40, ss. 5, 7. (2), Sch. 4 para. 68

Modifications etc. (not altering text)

C2. Pt. II applied in part (with modifications) (20.5.2016) by The Tobacco and Related Products Regulations 2016 (S.I. 2016/507), regs. 1. (2), 53. (3)

C42. Ss. 14-18 amended (3.10.1994) by S.I. 1994/2328, reg. 11. (b)

S. 17 excluded (1.1.1995) by S.I. 1994/2326, reg. 4. (1) (which said S.I. 1994/2326 was revoked (15.5.2002) by S.I. 2002/1144, reg. 1. (2), Sch. 11 para. 3)

S. 17 restricted (1.1.1995 until end of 1996) by S.I. 1994/2326, reg. 5

S. 17 restricted (24.2.1995) by S.I. 1995/204, reg. 10. (11)

S. 17 applied (with modifications) (9.1.1995) by S.I. 1994/3260, reg. 13. (1)

S. 17 excluded (7.6.2000) by S.I. 2000/1315, reg. 19. (2)

S. 17 restricted (13.6.2002) by S.I. 2002/618, reg. 62

S. 17 modified (13.6.2002) by S.I. 2002/618, reg. 63

S. 17 applied (with modifications) (15.5.2002) by S.I. 2002/1144, regs. 2. (2), 16. (1)-(3), Sch. 10 paras. 1, 3

C43. S. 17 applied (with modifications) (17.8.2015) by The Pyrotechnic Articles (Safety) Regulations 2015 (S.I. 2015/1553), reg. 1, Sch. 7 paras. 1. (d), 2

C44. S. 17 applied (with modifications) (8.12.2016) by The Electromagnetic Compatibility Regulations 2016 (S.I. 2016/1091), reg. 1, Sch. 7 paras. 1, 2 (with regs. 74, 75. (5))

C45. S. 17 applied (with modifications) (8.12.2016) by The Electrical Equipment (Safety) Regulations 2016 (S.I. 2016/1101), reg. 1, Sch. 3 paras. 1, 2 (with reg. 3)

C46. S. 17 applied (with modifications) (8.12.2016) by The Lifts Regulations 2016 (S.I. 2016/1093), reg. 1, Sch. 7 paras. 1. (d), 2 (with regs. 3-5)

C47. S. 17 applied (with modifications) (8.12.2016) by The Simple Pressure Vessels (Safety) Regulations 2016 (S.I. 2016/1092), reg. 1, Sch. 5 paras. 1. (d), 2 (with reg. 3)

C48. S. 17 applied (with modifications) (8.12.2016) by The Pressure Equipment (Safety) Regulations 2016 (S.I. 2016/1105), reg. 1, Sch. 7 paras. 1. (d), 2 (with reg. 88)
C49. S. 17 applied (with modifications) (3.8.2017) by The Recreational Craft Regulations 2017 (S.I. 2017/737), reg. 1, Sch. 13 paras. 1. (d), 2 (with reg. 89)
C50. S. 17 applied (with modifications) (26.12.2017) by The Radio Equipment Regulations 2017 (S.I. 2017/1206), reg. 1, Sch. 10 paras. 1, 2 (with regs. 3-5, 77)
Marginal Citations
M31975 c. 21.

18 Power to obtain information.

(1) If the Secretary of State considers that, for the purpose of deciding whether—
  (a) to make, vary or revoke any safety regulations; or
  (b) to serve, vary or revoke a prohibition notice; or
  (c) to serve or revoke a notice to warn,
he requires information which another person is likely to be able to furnish, the Secretary of State may serve on the other person a notice under this section.
(2) A notice served on any person under this section may require that person—
  (a) to furnish to the Secretary of State, within a period specified in the notice, such information as is so specified;
  (b) to produce such records as are specified in the notice at a time and place so specified and to permit a person appointed by the Secretary of State for the purpose to take copies of the records at that time and place.
(3) A person shall be guilty of an offence if he—
  (a) fails, without reasonable cause, to comply with a notice served on him under this section; or
  (b) in purporting to comply with a requirement which by virtue of paragraph (a) of subsection (2) above is contained in such a notice—
(i) furnishes information which he knows is false in a material particular; or
(ii) recklessly furnishes information which is false in a material particular.
(4) A person guilty of an offence under subsection (3) above shall—
  (a) in the case of an offence under paragraph (a) of that subsection, be liable on summary conviction to a fine not exceeding level 5 on the standard scale; and
  (b) in the case of an offence under paragraph (b) of that subsection be liable—
(i) on conviction on indictment, to a fine;
(ii) on summary conviction, to a fine not exceeding the statutory maximum.
Modifications etc. (not altering text)
C2. Pt. II applied in part (with modifications) (20.5.2016) by The Tobacco and Related Products Regulations 2016 (S.I. 2016/507), regs. 1. (2), 53. (3)
C51. Ss. 14-18 amended (3.10.1994) by S.I. 1994/2328, reg. 11. (b)
S. 18 applied (with modifications) (15.5.2002) by S.I. 2002/1144, regs. 2. (2), 16. (1)-(3), Sch. 10 paras. 1, 3
S. 18 applied (E.W.S.) (28.11.2003) by Fireworks Act 2003 (c. 22), ss. 2. (7), 18 (with s. 2. (8)); S.I. 2003/3084,{art. 2}, Sch.
C52. S. 18 applied (with modifications) (17.8.2015) by The Pyrotechnic Articles (Safety) Regulations 2015 (S.I. 2015/1553), reg. 1, Sch. 7 paras. 1. (e), 2
C53. S. 18 applied (with modifications) (8.12.2016) by The Pressure Equipment (Safety) Regulations 2016 (S.I. 2016/1105), reg. 1, Sch. 7 paras. 1. (e), 2 (with reg. 88)
C54. S. 18 applied (with modifications) (8.12.2016) by The Electromagnetic Compatibility Regulations 2016 (S.I. 2016/1091), reg. 1, Sch. 7 paras. 1, 2 (with regs. 74, 75. (5))
C55. S. 18 applied (with modifications) (8.12.2016) by The Electrical Equipment (Safety) Regulations 2016 (S.I. 2016/1101), reg. 1, Sch. 3 paras. 1, 2 (with reg. 3)
C56. S. 18 applied (with modifications) (8.12.2016) by The Simple Pressure Vessels (Safety)

Regulations 2016 (S.I. 2016/1092), reg. 1, Sch. 5 paras. 1. (e), 2 (with reg. 3)
C57. S. 18 applied (with modifications) (8.12.2016) by The Lifts Regulations 2016 (S.I. 2016/1093), reg. 1, Sch. 7 paras. 1. (e), 2 (with regs. 3-5)
C58. S. 18 applied (with modifications) (3.8.2017) by The Recreational Craft Regulations 2017 (S.I. 2017/737), reg. 1, Sch. 13 paras. 1. (e), 2 (with reg. 89)
C59. S. 18 applied (with modifications) (26.12.2017) by The Radio Equipment Regulations 2017 (S.I. 2017/1206), reg. 1, Sch. 10 paras. 1, 2 (with regs. 3-5, 77)
C60. S. 18. (1)(2): certain functions made exercisable concurrently (29.7.2004) by The Scotland Act 1998 (Transfer of Functions to the Scottish Ministers etc.) Order 2004 (S.I. 2004/2030), art. 4, Sch.

19 Interpretation of Part II.

(1) In this Part—
"controlled drug" means a controlled drug within the meaning of the M4. Misuse of Drugs Act 1971;
"feeding stuff" and "fertiliser" have the same meanings as in Part IV of the M5. Agriculture Act 1970;
"food" does not include anything containing tobacco but, subject to that, has the same meaning as in the [F10. Food Safety Act 1990] or, in relation to Northern Ireland, the same meaning as in the [F11. Food Safety (Northern Ireland) Order 1991];
"licensed medicinal product" means—
   (a) any medicinal product within the meaning of the M6. Medicines Act 1968 in respect of which a product licence within the meaning of that Act is for the time being in force; F12. . .
   (b) any other article or substance in respect of which any such licence is for the time being in force in pursuance of an order under section 104 or 105 of that Act (application of Act to other articles and substances); [F13or
   (c) a veterinary medicinal product that has a marketing authorisation under the Veterinary Medicines Regulations 2006.]
"safe", in relation to any goods, means such that there is no risk, or no risk apart from one reduced to a minimum, that any of the following will (whether immediately or after a definite or indefinite period) cause the death of, or any personal injury to, any person whatsoever, that is to say—
   (a) the goods;
   (b) the keeping, use or consumption of the goods;
   (c) the assembly of any of the goods which are, or are to be, supplied unassembled;
   (d) any emission or leakage from the goods or, as a result of the keeping, use or consumption of the goods, from anything else; or
   (e) reliance on the accuracy of any measurement, calculation or other reading made by or by means of the goods,
and F14. . . "unsafe" shall be construed accordingly;
"tobacco" includes any tobacco product within the meaning of the M7. Tobacco Products Duty Act 1979 and any article or substance containing tobacco and intended for oral or nasal use.
(2) In the definition of "safe" in subsection (1) above, references to the keeping, use or consumption of any goods are references to—
   (a) the keeping, use or consumption of the goods by the persons by whom, and in all or any of the ways or circumstances in which, they might reasonably be expected to be kept, used or consumed; and
   (b) the keeping, use or consumption of the goods either alone or in conjunction with other goods in conjunction with which they might reasonably be expected to be kept, used or consumed.
Amendments (Textual)
F10. In s. 19. (1) "Food Safety Act 1990" substituted (E.W.S.) for "Food Act 1984" by Food

Safety Act 1990 (c. 16, SIF 53:1, 2), s. 59. (1), Sch. 3 para. 37.
F11. Words in definition of "food" in s. 19. (1) substituted (N.I.) (21. 5.1991) by S.I. 1991/762, art. 51. (1), Sch. 2 para. 17; S.R. 1991/175, art. 2. (1).
F12. Word in s. 19. (1)(a) omitted (1.10.2006) by virtue of The Veterinary Medicines Regulations 2006 (S.I. 2006/2407), reg. 44. (3), Sch. 9 Pt. 1 para. 7. (a)
F13. S. 19. (1)(c) and word inserted (1.10.2006) by virtue of The Veterinary Medicines Regulations 2006 (S.I. 2006/2407), reg. 44. (3), Sch. 9 Pt. 1 para. 7. (b)
F14. Words in definition of "safe" in s. 19. (1) omitted (1.10.2005) by virtue of The General Product Safety Regulations 2005 (S.I. 2005/1803), reg. 46. (5) (with regs. 42, 43)
Modifications etc. (not altering text)
C2. Pt. II applied in part (with modifications) (20.5.2016) by The Tobacco and Related Products Regulations 2016 (S.I. 2016/507), regs. 1. (2), 53. (3)
C61. S. 19 modified (30.10.2005) by The Medicines (Traditional Herbal Medicinal Products for Human Use) Regulations 2005 (2005/2750), {reg. 10. (7)} (with Sch. 6)
C62. S. 19 applied (with modifications) (1.1.1995) by 1994/3144, reg. 9. (13) (as amended by S.I. 2005/2759, reg. 2. (12))
C63. S. 19 applied (with modifications) (8.12.2016) by The Electromagnetic Compatibility Regulations 2016 (S.I. 2016/1091), reg. 1, Sch. 7 paras. 1, 2 (with regs. 74, 75. (5))
C64. S. 19 applied (with modifications) (8.12.2016) by The Simple Pressure Vessels (Safety) Regulations 2016 (S.I. 2016/1092), reg. 1, Sch. 5 paras. 1. (f), 2 (with reg. 3)
C65. S. 19 applied (with modifications) (8.12.2016) by The Electrical Equipment (Safety) Regulations 2016 (S.I. 2016/1101), reg. 1, Sch. 3 paras. 1, 2 (with reg. 3)
C66. S. 19 applied (with modifications) (8.12.2016) by The Pressure Equipment (Safety) Regulations 2016 (S.I. 2016/1105), reg. 1, Sch. 7 paras. 1. (f), 2 (with reg. 88)
C67. S. 19 applied (with modifications) (3.8.2017) by The Recreational Craft Regulations 2017 (S.I. 2017/737), reg. 1, Sch. 13 paras. 1. (f), 2 (with reg. 89)
C68. S. 19. (1) modified (14.8.2012) by The Human Medicines Regulations 2012 (S.I. 2012/1916), reg. 1. (2), Sch. 34 para. 40 (with Sch. 32)
C69. S. 19: definition of "safe" applied (E.W.)(1.12.1991) by Water Industry Act 1991 (c. 56, SIF 130), ss. 74. (8), 223. (2)(savings in ss. 82. (3), 186. (1), 222. (1), Sch. 13 paras. 1, 2 and Sch. 14 para. 6)
Marginal Citations
M41971 c. 38.
M51970 c. 40.
M61968 c. 67.
M71979 c. 7.

Interpretation of Part II.

19 Interpretation of Part II.

(1) In this Part—
"controlled drug" means a controlled drug within the meaning of the M1. Misuse of Drugs Act 1971;
"feeding stuff" and "fertiliser" have the same meanings as in Part IV of the M2. Agriculture Act 1970;
"food" does not include anything containing tobacco but, subject to that, has the same meaning as in the [F1. Food Safety Act 1990] or, in relation to Northern Ireland, the same meaning as in the [F2. Food Safety (Northern Ireland) Order 1991];
"licensed medicinal product" means—

(a) any medicinal product within the meaning of the M3. Medicines Act 1968 in respect of which a product licence within the meaning of that Act is for the time being in force; F3. . .

(b) any other article or substance in respect of which any such licence is for the time being in force in pursuance of an order under section 104 or 105 of that Act (application of Act to other articles and substances); [F4or

(c) a veterinary medicinal product that has a marketing authorisation under the Veterinary Medicines Regulations 2006.]

"safe", in relation to any goods, means such that there is no risk, or no risk apart from one reduced to a minimum, that any of the following will (whether immediately or after a definite or indefinite period) cause the death of, or any personal injury to, any person whatsoever, that is to say—

(a) the goods;

(b) the keeping, use or consumption of the goods;

(c) the assembly of any of the goods which are, or are to be, supplied unassembled;

(d) any emission or leakage from the goods or, as a result of the keeping, use or consumption of the goods, from anything else; or

(e) reliance on the accuracy of any measurement, calculation or other reading made by or by means of the goods,

and F5. . . "unsafe" shall be construed accordingly;

"tobacco" includes any tobacco product within the meaning of the M4. Tobacco Products Duty Act 1979 and any article or substance containing tobacco and intended for oral or nasal use.

(2) In the definition of "safe" in subsection (1) above, references to the keeping, use or consumption of any goods are references to—

(a) the keeping, use or consumption of the goods by the persons by whom, and in all or any of the ways or circumstances in which, they might reasonably be expected to be kept, used or consumed; and

(b) the keeping, use or consumption of the goods either alone or in conjunction with other goods in conjunction with which they might reasonably be expected to be kept, used or consumed.

Amendments (Textual)

F1. In s. 19. (1) "Food Safety Act 1990" substituted (E.W.S.) for "Food Act 1984" by Food Safety Act 1990 (c. 16, SIF 53:1, 2), s. 59. (1), Sch. 3 para. 37.

F2. Words in definition of "food" in s. 19. (1) substituted (N.I.) (21. 5.1991) by S.I. 1991/762, art. 51. (1), Sch. 2 para. 17; S.R. 1991/175, art. 2. (1).

F3. Word in s. 19. (1)(a) omitted (1.10.2006) by virtue of The Veterinary Medicines Regulations 2006 (S.I. 2006/2407), reg. 44. (3), Sch. 9 Pt. 1 para. 7. (a)

F4. S. 19. (1)(c) and word inserted (1.10.2006) by virtue of The Veterinary Medicines Regulations 2006 (S.I. 2006/2407), reg. 44. (3), Sch. 9 Pt. 1 para. 7. (b)

F5. Words in definition of "safe" in s. 19. (1) omitted (1.10.2005) by virtue of The General Product Safety Regulations 2005 (S.I. 2005/1803), reg. 46. (5) (with regs. 42, 43)

Modifications etc. (not altering text)

C1. Pt. II applied in part (with modifications) (20.5.2016) by The Tobacco and Related Products Regulations 2016 (S.I. 2016/507), regs. 1. (2), 53. (3)

C2. S. 19 modified (30.10.2005) by The Medicines (Traditional Herbal Medicinal Products for Human Use) Regulations 2005 (2005/2750), {reg. 10. (7)} (with Sch. 6)

C3. S. 19 applied (with modifications) (1.1.1995) by 1994/3144, reg. 9. (13) (as amended by S.I. 2005/2759, reg. 2. (12))

C4. S. 19 applied (with modifications) (8.12.2016) by The Electromagnetic Compatibility Regulations 2016 (S.I. 2016/1091), reg. 1, Sch. 7 paras. 1, 2 (with regs. 74, 75. (5))

C5. S. 19 applied (with modifications) (8.12.2016) by The Simple Pressure Vessels (Safety) Regulations 2016 (S.I. 2016/1092), reg. 1, Sch. 5 paras. 1. (f), 2 (with reg. 3)

C6. S. 19 applied (with modifications) (8.12.2016) by The Electrical Equipment (Safety) Regulations 2016 (S.I. 2016/1101), reg. 1, Sch. 3 paras. 1, 2 (with reg. 3)

C7. S. 19 applied (with modifications) (8.12.2016) by The Pressure Equipment (Safety)

Regulations 2016 (S.I. 2016/1105), reg. 1, Sch. 7 paras. 1. (f), 2 (with reg. 88)
C8. S. 19 applied (with modifications) (3.8.2017) by The Recreational Craft Regulations 2017 (S.I. 2017/737), reg. 1, Sch. 13 paras. 1. (f), 2 (with reg. 89)
C9. S. 19. (1) modified (14.8.2012) by The Human Medicines Regulations 2012 (S.I. 2012/1916), reg. 1. (2), Sch. 34 para. 40 (with Sch. 32)
C10. S. 19: definition of "safe" applied (E.W.)(1.12.1991) by Water Industry Act 1991 (c. 56, SIF 130), ss. 74. (8), 223. (2)(savings in ss. 82. (3), 186. (1), 222. (1), Sch. 13 paras. 1, 2 and Sch. 14 para. 6)
Marginal Citations
M1 1971 c. 38.
M2 1970 c. 40.
M3 1968 c. 67.
M4 1979 c. 7.

Part III Misleading Price Indications

Part III Misleading Price Indications

20 Offence of giving misleading indication.

F1. . . . .
Amendments (Textual)
F1. Ss. 20-26 repealed (26.5.2008) by The Consumer Protection from Unfair Trading Regulations 2008 (S.I. 2008/1277), reg. 30, Sch. 2 para. 34, Sch. 4 (with reg. 28. (2)(3), Sch. 3 para. 5)

21 Meaning of "misleading".

F2. . . . .
Amendments (Textual)
F2. Ss. 20-26 repealed (26.5.2008) by The Consumer Protection from Unfair Trading Regulations 2008 (S.I. 2008/1277), reg. 30, Sch. 2 para. 34, Sch. 4 (with reg. 28. (2)(3), Sch. 3 para. 5)

22 Application to provision of services and facilities.

F3. . . . .
Amendments (Textual)
F3. Ss. 20-26 repealed (26.5.2008) by The Consumer Protection from Unfair Trading Regulations 2008 (S.I. 2008/1277), reg. 30, Sch. 2 para. 34, Sch. 4 (with reg. 28. (2)(3), Sch. 3 para. 5)

23 Application to provision of accommodation etc.

F4. . . . .
Amendments (Textual)
F4. Ss. 20-26 repealed (26.5.2008) by The Consumer Protection from Unfair Trading Regulations 2008 (S.I. 2008/1277), reg. 30, Sch. 2 para. 34, Sch. 4 (with reg. 28. (2)(3), Sch. 3 para. 5)

24 Defences.

F5. . . . .
Amendments (Textual)
F5. Ss. 20-26 repealed (26.5.2008) by The Consumer Protection from Unfair Trading Regulations 2008 (S.I. 2008/1277), reg. 30, Sch. 2 para. 34, Sch. 4 (with reg. 28. (2)(3), Sch. 3 para. 5)

25 Code of practice.

F6. . . . .
Amendments (Textual)
F6. Ss. 20-26 repealed (26.5.2008) by The Consumer Protection from Unfair Trading Regulations 2008 (S.I. 2008/1277), reg. 30, Sch. 2 para. 34, Sch. 4 (with reg. 28. (2)(3), Sch. 3 para. 5)

26 Power to make regulations.

F7. . . . .
Amendments (Textual)
F7. Ss. 20-26 repealed (26.5.2008) by The Consumer Protection from Unfair Trading Regulations 2008 (S.I. 2008/1277), reg. 30, Sch. 2 para. 34, Sch. 4 (with reg. 28. (2)(3), Sch. 3 para. 5)

Part IV Enforcement of Parts II and III

Part IV Enforcement of Parts II and III

Modifications etc. (not altering text)
C1. Pt. IV (ss. 27-35) applied (1.1.1993) by S.I. 1992/3139, reg. 3. (2)(c) (which said S.I. 1992/3139 was revoked (15.5.2002) by S.I. 2002/1144, reg. 1. (2), Sch. 11 para. 1)
C2. Pt. IV applied in part (with modifications) (20.5.2016) by The Tobacco and Related Products Regulations 2016 (S.I. 2016/507), regs. 1. (2), 53. (3)

27 Enforcement.

(1) Subject to the following provisions of this section—
   (a) it shall be the duty of every weights and measures authority in Great Britain to enforce within their area the safety provisions F1. . . ; and
   (b) it shall be the duty of every district council in Northern Ireland to enforce within their area the safety provisions.
(2) The Secretary of State may by regulations—
   (a) wholly or partly transfer any duty imposed by subsection (1) above on a weights and measures authority or a district council in Northern Ireland to such other person who has agreed to the transfer as is specified in the regulations;
   (b) relieve such an authority or council of any such duty so far as it is exercisable in relation to such goods as may be described in the regulations.
(3) The power to make regulations under subsection (2) above shall be exercisable by statutory instrument subject to annulment in pursuance of a resolution of either House of Parliament and shall include power—
   (a) to make different provision for different cases; and
   (b) to make such supplemental, consequential and transitional provision as the Secretary of State considers appropriate.

[F2. (3. A)For the investigatory powers available to a person for the purposes of the duty imposed by subsection (1), see Schedule 5 to the Consumer Rights Act 2015 (as well as section 29).]

(4) Nothing in this section shall authorise any weights and measures authority, or any person on whom functions are conferred by regulations under subsection (2) above, to bring proceedings in Scotland for an offence.

Amendments (Textual)

F1. Words in s. 27. (1)(a) repealed (26.5.2008) by The Consumer Protection from Unfair Trading Regulations 2008 (S.I. 2008/1277), reg. 30. (3), Sch. 4 Pt. 1 (with reg. 28. (2)(3), Sch. 3 para. 6)

F2. S. 27. (3. A) inserted (1.10.2015) by Consumer Rights Act 2015 (c. 15), s. 100. (5), Sch. 6 para. 38; S.I. 2015/1630, art. 3. (i) (with art. 8)

Modifications etc. (not altering text)

C3. S. 27 applied (in part) (E.W.S.) (28.11.2003 for certain purposes, 15.7.2004 for certain further purposes and otherwise prosp.) by (Fireworks Act 2003 (c. 22), ss. 12. (1), 18 (with s. 2. (8)); S.I. 2003/3084, art. 2, Sch.; S.I. 2004/1831, art.2, Sch.

C4. Functions under s. 27. (2)(3) made exercisable concurrently (29.7.2004 for certain purposes) by The Scotland Act 1998 (Transfer of Functions to the Scottish Ministers etc.) Order 2004 (S.I. 2004/2030), art. 4, Sch.

F3 28 Test purchases.

. . . .

Amendments (Textual)

F3. S. 28 omitted (1.10.2015) by virtue of Consumer Rights Act 2015 (c. 15), s. 100. (5), Sch. 6 para. 39; S.I. 2015/1630, art. 3. (i) (with art. 8)

Modifications etc. (not altering text)

C5. S. 28 applied (with modifications) (1.1.1993) by S.I. 1992/3073, reg. 28, Sch. 6 para. 3. (c).
S. 28 applied (with modifications) (1.7.1997) by S.I. 1997/831, reg. 19. (1)-(4), Sch. 15 para. 2. (b) (with Sch. 15 para. 7)
Ss. 28-35 applied (with modifications) (31.5.1998) by S.I. 1998/1165, reg. 13. (2)(a) (which said S.I. was revoked (25.8.2003) by S.I. 2003/1941, reg. 1. (2))
Ss. 28-35 applied (with modifications) (26.4.1999) by S.I. 1999/1053, reg. 16. (3)(a)
Ss. 28-35 applied (with modifications) (29.11.1999) by S.I. 1999/2001, reg. 24, Sch. 8 para. 2. (c)
Ss. 28-35 applied (with modifications) (8.4.2000) by S.I. 2000/730, reg. 18. (1), Sch. 9 para. 1. (2)
Ss. 28-35 applied (with modifications) (15.5.2002) by S.I. 2002/1144, regs. 2. (2), 16. (1)-(3), Sch. 10 paras. 1, 3
Ss. 28-35 applied (with modifications) (25.8.2003) by S.I. 2003/1941, reg. 8, Sch. IV para. 2. (a)
C6. S. 28 applied (with modifications) (17.8.2015) by The Pyrotechnic Articles (Safety) Regulations 2015 (S.I. 2015/1553), reg. 1, Sch. 7 paras. 1. (f), 2

29 Powers of search etc.

(1) Subject to the following provisions of this Part, a duly authorised officer of an enforcement authority may at any reasonable hour and on production, if required, of his credentials exercise [F4the power conferred by subsection (4)].

F5. (2). . . . .

F6. (3). . . . .

(4) If the officer has reasonable grounds for suspecting that any goods are manufactured or imported goods which have not been supplied in the United Kingdom since they were manufactured or imported he may—

(a) for the purpose of ascertaining whether there has been any contravention of any safety provision in relation to the goods, require any person carrying on a business, or employed in connection with a business, to produce any records relating to the business;

(b) for the purpose of ascertaining (by testing or otherwise) whether there has been any such contravention, seize and detain the goods;

(c) take copies of, or of any entry in, any records produced by virtue of paragraph (a) above.

F7. (5). . . . .

F8. (6). . . . .

(7) If and to the extent that it is reasonably necessary to do so to prevent a contravention of any safety provision F9. . . , the officer may, for the purpose of exercising his power under subsection (4)F10... above to seize any goods F11...—

(a) require any person having authority to do so to open any container or to open any vending machine; and

(b) himself open or break open any such container or machine where a requirement made under paragraph (a) above in relation to the container or machine has not been complied with.

Amendments (Textual)

F4. Words in s. 29. (1) substituted (1.10.2015) by Consumer Rights Act 2015 (c. 15), s. 100. (5), Sch. 6 para. 40. (2); S.I. 2015/1630, art. 3. (i) (with art. 8)

F5. S. 29. (2) omitted (1.10.2015) by virtue of Consumer Rights Act 2015 (c. 15), s. 100. (5), Sch. 6 para. 40. (3); S.I. 2015/1630, art. 3. (i) (with art. 8)

F6. S. 29. (3) omitted (1.10.2015) by virtue of Consumer Rights Act 2015 (c. 15), s. 100. (5), Sch. 6 para. 40. (3); S.I. 2015/1630, art. 3. (i) (with art. 8)

F7. S. 29. (5) omitted (1.10.2015) by virtue of Consumer Rights Act 2015 (c. 15), s. 100. (5), Sch. 6 para. 40. (3); S.I. 2015/1630, art. 3. (i) (with art. 8)

F8. S. 29. (6) omitted (1.10.2015) by virtue of Consumer Rights Act 2015 (c. 15), s. 100. (5), Sch. 6 para. 40. (3); S.I. 2015/1630, art. 3. (i) (with art. 8)

F9. Words in s. 29. (7) repealed (26.5.2008) by The Consumer Protection from Unfair Trading Regulations 2008 (S.I. 2008/1277), reg. 30. (3), Sch. 4 Pt. 1 (with reg. 28. (2)(3), Sch. 3 para. 6)

F10. Words in s. 29. (7) omitted (1.10.2015) by virtue of Consumer Rights Act 2015 (c. 15), s. 100. (5), Sch. 6 para. 40. (4)(a); S.I. 2015/1630, art. 3. (i) (with art. 8)

F11. Words in s. 29. (7) omitted (1.10.2015) by virtue of Consumer Rights Act 2015 (c. 15), s. 100. (5), Sch. 6 para. 40. (4)(b); S.I. 2015/1630, art. 3. (i) (with art. 8)

Modifications etc. (not altering text)

C7. S. 29 applied (with modifications) (1.1.1993) by S.I. 1992/3073, reg. 28, Sch. 6 para. 3. (c)

S. 29 applied (with modifications) (1.7.1997) by S.I. 1997/831, reg. 19. (1)-(4), Sch. 15 para. 2. (b) (with Sch. 15 para. 7)

Ss. 28-35 applied (with modifications) (31.5.1998) by S.I. 1998/1165, reg. 13. (2)(a) (which said S.I. was revoked (25.8.2003) by S.I. 2003/1941, reg. 1. (2))

Ss. 28-35 applied (with modifications) (26.4.1999) by S.I. 1999/1053, reg. 16. (3)(a)

Ss. 28-35 applied (with modifications) (29.11.1999) by S.I. 1999/2001, reg. 24, Sch. 8 para. 2. (c)

Ss. 28-35 applied (with modifications) (8.4.2000) by S.I. 2000/730, reg. 18. (1), Sch. 9 para. 1. (2)

Ss. 28-35 applied (with modifications) (15.5.2002) by S.I. 2002/1144, regs. 2. (2), 16. (1)-(3), Sch. 10 paras. 1, 3

Ss. 28-35 applied (with modifications) (25.8.2003) by S.I. 2003/1941, reg. 8, Sch. IV para. 2. (a)

C8. S. 29 applied (with modifications) (17.8.2015) by The Pyrotechnic Articles (Safety) Regulations 2015 (S.I. 2015/1553), reg. 1, Sch. 7 paras. 1. (g), 2

C9. S. 29 applied (with modifications) (8.12.2016) by The Simple Pressure Vessels (Safety) Regulations 2016 (S.I. 2016/1092), reg. 1, Sch. 5 paras. 1. (g), 2 (with reg. 3)

C10. S. 29 applied (with modifications) (8.12.2016) by The Pressure Equipment (Safety) Regulations 2016 (S.I. 2016/1105), reg. 1, Sch. 7 paras. 1. (g), 2 (with reg. 88)

C11. S. 29 applied (with modifications) (8.12.2016) by The Electromagnetic Compatibility Regulations 2016 (S.I. 2016/1091), reg. 1, Sch. 7 paras. 1, 2 (with regs. 74, 75. (5))

C12. S. 29 applied (with modifications) (8.12.2016) by The Electrical Equipment (Safety) Regulations 2016 (S.I. 2016/1101), reg. 1, Sch. 3 paras. 1, 2 (with reg. 3)

C13. S. 29 applied (with modifications) (8.12.2016) by The Lifts Regulations 2016 (S.I. 2016/1093), reg. 1, Sch. 7 paras. 1. (f), 2 (with regs. 3-5)

C14. S. 29 applied (with modifications) (3.8.2017) by The Recreational Craft Regulations 2017 (S.I. 2017/737), reg. 1, Sch. 13 paras. 1. (g), 2 (with reg. 89)

C15. S. 29 applied (with modifications) (26.12.2017) by The Radio Equipment Regulations 2017 (S.I. 2017/1206), reg. 1, Sch. 10 paras. 1, 2 (with regs. 3-5, 77)

C16. S. 29. (1)-(5)(6)(a)(7) applied in part (E.W.S) (28.11.2003 for certain purposes, 15.7.2004 for certain further purposes and otherwise prosp.) by Fireworks Act 2003 (c. 22), ss. 12. (2)(b), 18 (with s. 2. (8)); S.I. 2003/3084, art. 2, Sch.; S.I. 2004/1831, art. 2, Sch.

C17. S. 29. (4)(5)(6): powers of seizure extended (1.4.2003) by 2001 c. 16, ss. 50, 52-55, 68, 138. (2), Sch. 1 Pt. 1 para. 45; S.I. 2003/708, art. 2. (j)

30 Provisions supplemental to s. 29.

(1) An officer seizing any goods F12... under section [F1329. (4)] above shall inform the following persons that the goods F12... have been so seized, that is to say—
  (a) the person from whom they are seized; and
  (b) in the case of imported goods seized on any premises under the control of the
Commissioners of Customs and Excise, the importer of those goods (within the meaning of the M1. Customs and Excise Management Act 1979).

(2) If a justice of the peace—
  (a) is satisfied by any written information on oath that there are reasonable grounds for believing either—
(i) that any F14... records which any officer has power to inspect under section [F1529. (4)] above are on any premises and that their inspection is likely to disclose evidence that there has been a contravention of any safety provision F16. . . ; or
(ii) that such a contravention has taken place, is taking place or is about to take place on any premises; and
  (b) is also satisfied by any such information either—
(i) that admission to the premises has been or is likely to be refused and that notice of intention to apply for a warrant under this subsection has been given to the occupier; or
(ii) that an application for admission, or the giving of such a notice, would defeat the object of the entry or that the premises are unoccupied or that the occupier is temporarily absent and it might defeat the object of the entry to await his return,
the justice may by warrant under his hand, which shall continue in force for a period of one month, authorise any officer of an enforcement authority to enter the premises, if need be by force.

(3) An officer entering any premises by virtue of F17... a warrant under subsection (2) above may take with him such other persons and such equipment as may appear to him necessary.

(4) On leaving any premises which a person is authorised to enter by a warrant under subsection (2) above, that person shall, if the premises are unoccupied or the occupier is temporarily absent, leave the premises as effectively secured against trespassers as he found them.

(5) If any person who is not an officer of an enforcement authority purports to act as such under section [F1829. (4)] above or this section he shall be guilty of an offence and liable on summary conviction to a fine not exceeding level 5 on the standard scale.

(6) Where any goods seized by an officer under section [F1929. (4)] above are submitted to a test, the officer shall inform the persons mentioned in subsection (1) above of the result of the test and, if—
  (a) proceedings are brought for an offence in respect of a contravention in relation to the goods of any safety provision F20. . . or for the forfeiture of the goods under section 16 or 17 above, or a suspension notice is served in respect of any goods; and
  (b) the officer is requested to do so and it is practicable to comply with the request,
the officer shall allow any person who is a party to the proceedings or, as the case may be, has an interest in the goods to which the notice relates to have the goods tested.

(7) The Secretary of State may by regulations provide that any test of goods seized under section

[F2129. (4)] above by an officer of an enforcement authority shall—
  (a) be carried out at the expense of the authority in a manner and by a person prescribed by or determined under the regulations; or
  (b) be carried out either as mentioned in paragraph (a) above or by the authority in a manner prescribed by the regulations.
(8) The power to make regulations under subsection (7) above shall be exercisable by statutory instrument subject to annulment in pursuance of a resolution of either House of Parliament and shall include power—
  (a) to make different provision for different cases; and
  (b) to make such supplemental, consequential and transitional provision as the Secretary of State considers appropriate.
(9) In the application of this section to Scotland, the reference in subsection (2) above to a justice of the peace shall include a reference to a sheriff and the references to written information on oath shall be construed as references to evidence on oath.
(10) In the application of this section to Northern Ireland, the references in subsection (2) above to any information on oath shall be construed as references to any complaint on oath.

Amendments (Textual)
F12. Words in s. 30. (1) omitted (1.10.2015) by virtue of Consumer Rights Act 2015 (c. 15), s. 100. (5), Sch. 6 para. 41. (2)(b); S.I. 2015/1630, art. 3. (i) (with art. 8)
F13. Word in s. 30. (1) substituted (1.10.2015) by Consumer Rights Act 2015 (c. 15), s. 100. (5), Sch. 6 para. 41. (2)(a); S.I. 2015/1630, art. 3. (i) (with art. 8)
F14. Words in s. 30. (2)(a)(i) omitted (1.10.2015) by virtue of Consumer Rights Act 2015 (c. 15), s. 100. (5), Sch. 6 para. 41. (3)(a); S.I. 2015/1630, art. 3. (i) (with art. 8)
F15. Word in s. 30. (2)(a)(i) substituted (1.10.2015) by Consumer Rights Act 2015 (c. 15), s. 100. (5), Sch. 6 para. 41. (3)(b); S.I. 2015/1630, art. 3. (i) (with art. 8)
F16. Words in s. 30. (2)(a)(i) repealed (26.5.2008) by The Consumer Protection from Unfair Trading Regulations 2008 (S.I. 2008/1277), reg. 30. (3), Sch. 4 Pt. 1 (with reg. 28. (2)(3), Sch. 3 para. 6)
F17. Words in s. 30. (3) omitted (1.10.2015) by virtue of Consumer Rights Act 2015 (c. 15), s. 100. (5), Sch. 6 para. 41. (4); S.I. 2015/1630, art. 3. (i) (with art. 8)
F18. Word in s. 30. (5) substituted (1.10.2015) by Consumer Rights Act 2015 (c. 15), s. 100. (5), Sch. 6 para. 41. (5); S.I. 2015/1630, art. 3. (i) (with art. 8)
F19. Word in s. 30. (6) substituted (1.10.2015) by Consumer Rights Act 2015 (c. 15), s. 100. (5), Sch. 6 para. 41. (5); S.I. 2015/1630, art. 3. (i) (with art. 8)
F20. Words in s. 30. (6)(a) repealed (26.5.2008) by The Consumer Protection from Unfair Trading Regulations 2008 (S.I. 2008/1277), reg. 30. (3), Sch. 4 Pt. 1 (with reg. 28. (2)(3), Sch. 3 para. 6)
F21. Word in s. 30. (7) substituted (1.10.2015) by Consumer Rights Act 2015 (c. 15), s. 100. (5), Sch. 6 para. 41. (5); S.I. 2015/1630, art. 3. (i) (with art. 8)

Modifications etc. (not altering text)
C18. S. 30 applied (with modifications) (1.1.1993) by S.I. 1992/3073, reg. 28, Sch. 6 para. 3. (c).
S. 30 applied (with modifications) (1.7.1997) by S.I. 1997/831, reg. 19. (1)-(4), Sch. 15 para. 2 (b) (with Sch. 15 para. 7)
Ss. 28-35 applied (with modifications) (31.5.1998) by S.I. 1998/1165, reg. 13. (2)(a) (which said S.I. was revoked (25.8.2003) by S.I. 2003/1941, reg. 1. (2))
Ss. 28-35 applied (with modifications) (26.4.1999) by S.I. 1999/1053, reg. 16. (3)(a)
Ss. 28-35 applied (with modifications) (29.11.1999) by S.I. 1999/2001, reg. 24, Sch. 8 para. 2. (c)
Ss. 28-35 applied (with modifications) (8.4.2000) by S.I. 2000/730, reg. 18. (1), Sch. 9 para. 1. (2)
Ss. 28-35 applied (with modifications) (15.5.2002) by S.I. 2002/1144, regs. 2. (2), 16. (1)-(3), Sch. 10 paras. 1, 3
Ss. 28-35 applied (with modifications) (25.8.2003) by S.I. 2003/1941, reg. 8, Sch. IV para. 2. (a)
C19. S. 30 applied (with modifications) (17.8.2015) by The Pyrotechnic Articles (Safety) Regulations 2015 (S.I. 2015/1553), reg. 1, Sch. 7 paras. 1. (h), 2
C20. S. 30 applied (with modifications) (8.12.2016) by The Electromagnetic Compatibility

Regulations 2016 (S.I. 2016/1091), reg. 1, Sch. 7 paras. 1, 2 (with regs. 74, 75. (5))
C21. S. 30 applied (with modifications) (8.12.2016) by The Pressure Equipment (Safety) Regulations 2016 (S.I. 2016/1105), reg. 1, Sch. 7 paras. 1. (h), 2 (with reg. 88)
C22. S. 30 applied (with modifications) (8.12.2016) by The Simple Pressure Vessels (Safety) Regulations 2016 (S.I. 2016/1092), reg. 1, Sch. 5 paras. 1. (h), 2 (with reg. 3)
C23. S. 30 applied (with modifications) (8.12.2016) by The Electrical Equipment (Safety) Regulations 2016 (S.I. 2016/1101), reg. 1, Sch. 3 paras. 1, 2 (with reg. 3)
C24. S. 30 applied (with modifications) (8.12.2016) by The Lifts Regulations 2016 (S.I. 2016/1093), reg. 1, Sch. 7 paras. 1. (g), 2 (with regs. 3-5)
C25. S. 30 applied (with modifications) (3.8.2017) by The Recreational Craft Regulations 2017 (S.I. 2017/737), reg. 1, Sch. 13 paras. 1. (h), 2 (with reg. 89)
C26. S. 30 applied (with modifications) (26.12.2017) by The Radio Equipment Regulations 2017 (S.I. 2017/1206), reg. 1, Sch. 10 paras. 1, 2 (with regs. 3-5, 77)
C27. S. 30. (1)-(9) applied (E.W.S) (28.11.2003 for certain purposes , 15.7.2004 for certain futher purposes and otherwise prosp.) by Fireworks Act 2003 (c. 22), ss. 12. (2)(b), 18 (with s. 2. (8)); S.I. 2003/3084, art. 2, Sch.; S.I. 2004/1831, art. 2, Sch.
C28. S. 30. (6)(7) applied (1.4.2003) by 2001 c. 16, ss. 70, 138. (2), Sch. 2 Pt. 1 para. 3; S.I. 2003/708, art. 2. (k)
Marginal Citations
M1 1979 c. 2.

31 Power of customs officer to detain goods.

(1) A customs officer may, for the purpose of facilitating the exercise by an enforcement authority or officer of such an authority of any functions conferred on the authority or officer by or under Part II of this Act, or by [F22section 29. (4) of this Act or Schedule 5 to the Consumer Rights Act 2015] in its application for the purposes of the safety provisions, seize any imported goods and detain them for not more than two working days.
(2) Anything seized and detained under this section shall be dealt with during the period of its detention in such manner as the Commissioners of Customs and Excise may direct.
(3) In subsection (1) above the reference to two working days is a reference to a period of forty-eight hours calculated from the time when the goods in question are seized but disregarding so much of any period as falls on a Saturday or Sunday or on Christmas Day, Good Friday or a day which is a bank holiday under the M2. Banking and Financial Dealings Act 1971 in the part of the United Kingdom where the goods are seized.
(4) In this section and section 32 below "customs officer" means any officer within the meaning of the M3. Customs and Excise Management Act 1979.
Amendments (Textual)
F22. Words in s. 31. (1) substituted (1.10.2015) by Consumer Rights Act 2015 (c. 15), s. 100. (5), Sch. 6 para. 42; S.I. 2015/1630, art. 3. (i) (with art. 8)
Modifications etc. (not altering text)
C29. S. 31 applied (with modifications) (1.1.1993) by S.I. 1992/3073, reg. 28, Sch. 6 para. 3. (c)
S. 31 applied (with modifications) (1.7.1997) by S.I. 1997/831, reg. 19. (1)-(4), Sch. 15 para. 2. (b) (with Sch. 15 para. 7)
Ss. 28-35 applied (with modifications) (31.5.1998) by S.I. 1998/1165, reg. 13. (2)(a) (which said S.I. was revoked (25.8.2003) by S.I. 2003/1941, reg. 1. (2))
Ss. 28-35 applied (with modifications) (26.4.1999) by S.I. 1999/1053, reg. 16. (3)(a)
Ss. 28-35 applied (with modifications) (29.11.1999) by S.I. 1999/2001, reg. 24, Sch. 8 para. 2. (c)
Ss. 28-35 applied (with modifications) (8.4.2000) by S.I. 2000/730, reg. 18. (1), Sch. 9 para. 1. (2)
Ss. 28-35 applied (with modifications) (15.5.2002) by S.I. 2002/1144, regs. 2. (2), 16. (1)-(3), Sch. 10 paras. 1, 3
Ss. 28-35 applied (with modifications) (25.8.2003) by S.I. 2003/1941, reg. 8, Sch. IV para. 2. (a)

C30. S. 31 applied (with modifications) (17.8.2015) by The Pyrotechnic Articles (Safety) Regulations 2015 (S.I. 2015/1553), reg. 1, Sch. 7 paras. 1. (i), 2
C31. S. 31 applied (with modifications) (1.10.2015) by The Packaging (Essential Requirements) Regulations 2015 (S.I. 2015/1640), reg. 1, Sch. 4 para. 1. (1)(a) (with reg. 3. (5))
C32. S. 31 applied (with modifications) (8.12.2016) by The Lifts Regulations 2016 (S.I. 2016/1093), reg. 1, Sch. 7 paras. 1. (h), 2 (with regs. 3-5)
C33. S. 31 applied (with modifications) (8.12.2016) by The Simple Pressure Vessels (Safety) Regulations 2016 (S.I. 2016/1092), reg. 1, Sch. 5 paras. 1. (i), 2 (with reg. 3)
C34. S. 31 applied (with modifications) (8.12.2016) by The Electromagnetic Compatibility Regulations 2016 (S.I. 2016/1091), reg. 1, Sch. 7 paras. 1, 2 (with regs. 74, 75. (5))
C35. S. 31 applied (with modifications) (8.12.2016) by The Pressure Equipment (Safety) Regulations 2016 (S.I. 2016/1105), reg. 1, Sch. 7 paras. 1. (i), 2 (with reg. 88)
C36. S. 31 applied (with modifications) (8.12.2016) by The Electrical Equipment (Safety) Regulations 2016 (S.I. 2016/1101), reg. 1, Sch. 3 paras. 1, 2 (with reg. 3)
C37. S. 31 applied (with modifications) (3.8.2017) by The Recreational Craft Regulations 2017 (S.I. 2017/737), reg. 1, Sch. 13 paras. 1. (i), 2 (with reg. 89)
C38. S. 31 applied (with modifications) (26.12.2017) by The Radio Equipment Regulations 2017 (S.I. 2017/1206), reg. 1, Sch. 10 paras. 1, 2 (with regs. 3-5, 77)
Marginal Citations
M21971 c. 80.
M31979 c. 2.

32 Obstruction of authorised officer.

(1) Any person who—
(a) intentionally obstructs any officer of an enforcement authority who is acting in pursuance of [F23section 29. (4)] or any customs officer who is [F24acting in pursuance of section 31]; or
(b) intentionally fails to comply with any requirement made of him by any officer of an enforcement authority under [F25section 29. (4)]; or
(c) without reasonable cause fails to give any officer of an enforcement authority who is so acting any other assistance or information which the officer may reasonably require of him for the purposes of the exercise of the officer's functions under [F26section 29. (4)],
shall be guilty of an offence and liable on summary conviction to a fine not exceeding level 5 on the standard scale.
(2) A person shall be guilty of an offence if, in giving any information which is required of him by virtue of subsection (1)(c) above—
(a) he makes any statement which he knows is false in a material particular; or
(b) he recklessly makes a statement which is false in a material particular.
(3) A person guilty of an offence under subsection (2) above shall be liable—
(a) on conviction on indictment, to a fine;
(b) on summary conviction, to a fine not exceeding the statutory maximum.
Amendments (Textual)
F23. Words in s. 32. (1)(a) substituted (1.10.2015) by Consumer Rights Act 2015 (c. 15), s. 100. (5), Sch. 6 para. 43. (a)(i); S.I. 2015/1630, art. 3. (i) (with art. 8)
F24. Words in s. 32. (1)(a) substituted (1.10.2015) by Consumer Rights Act 2015 (c. 15), s. 100. (5), Sch. 6 para. 43. (a)(ii); S.I. 2015/1630, art. 3. (i) (with art. 8)
F25. Words in s. 32. (1)(b) substituted (1.10.2015) by Consumer Rights Act 2015 (c. 15), s. 100. (5), Sch. 6 para. 43. (b); S.I. 2015/1630, art. 3. (i) (with art. 8)
F26. Words in s. 32. (1)(c) substituted (1.10.2015) by Consumer Rights Act 2015 (c. 15), s. 100. (5), Sch. 6 para. 43. (c); S.I. 2015/1630, art. 3. (i) (with art. 8)
Modifications etc. (not altering text)
C39. S. 32 applied (E.W.S) (28.11.2003 for certain purposes, 15.7.2004 for certain further

purposes and otherwise prosp.) by Fireworks Act 2003 (c. 22), ss. 12. (2)(c), 18 (with s. 2. (8));
S.I. 2003/3084, art. 2, Sch.; S.I. 2004/1831, art. 2, Sch.
C40. S. 32 applied (with modifications) (1.1.1993) by S.I. 1992/3073, reg. 28, Sch. 6 para. 3. (c)
S. 32 applied (with modifications) (1.7.1997) by S.I. 1997/831, reg. 19. (1)-(4), Sch. 15 para. 2.
(b) (with Sch. 15 para. 7)
Ss. 28-35 applied (with modifications) (31.5.1998) by S.I. 1998/1165, reg. 13. (2)(a) (which said
S.I. was revoked (25.8.2003) by S.I. 2003/1941, reg. 1. (2))
Ss. 28-35 applied (with modifications) (29.11.1999) by S.I. 1999/2001, reg. 24, Sch. 8 para. 2. (c)
Ss. 28-35 applied (with modifications) (26.4.1999) by S.I. 1999/1053, reg. 16. (3)(a)
Ss. 28-35 applied (with modifications) (8.4.2000) by S.I. 2000/730, reg. 18. (1), Sch. 9 para. 1. (2)
Ss. 28-35 applied (with modifications) (15.5.2002) by S.I. 2002/1144, regs. 2. (2), 16. (1)-(3), Sch.
10 paras. 1, 3
Ss. 28-35 applied (with modifications) (25.8.2003) by S.I. 2003/1941, reg. 8, Sch. IV para. 2. (a)
C41. S. 32 applied (with modifications) (1.10.2015) by The Packaging (Essential Requirements)
Regulations 2015 (S.I. 2015/1640), reg. 1, Sch. 4 para. 1. (1)(a) (with reg. 3. (5))

33 Appeals against detention of goods.

(1) Any person having an interest in any goods which are for the time being detained under
[F27section 29. (4)] by an enforcement authority or by an officer of such an authority may apply
for an order requiring the goods to be released to him or to another person.
(2) An application under this section may be made—
   (a) to any magistrates' court in which proceedings have been brought in England and Wales or
Northern Ireland—
(i) for an offence in respect of a contravention in relation to the goods of any safety provision F28.
. . ; or
(ii) for the forfeiture of the goods under section 16 above;
   (b) where no such proceedings have been so brought, by way of complaint to a magistrates'
court; or
   (c) in Scotland, by summary application to the sheriff.
(3) On an application under this section to a magistrates' court or to the sheriff, an order requiring
goods to be released shall be made only if the court or sheriff is satisfied—
   (a) that proceedings—
(i) for an offence in respect of a contravention in relation to the goods of any safety provision F29.
. . ; or
(ii) for the forfeiture of the goods under section 16 or 17 above,
have not been brought or, having been brought, have been concluded without the goods being
forfeited; and
   (b) where no such proceedings have been brought, that more than six months have elapsed since
the goods were seized.
(4) Any person aggrieved by an order made under this section by a magistrates' court in England
and Wales or Northern Ireland, or by a decision of such a court not to make such an order, may
appeal against that order or decision—
   (a) in England and Wales, to the Crown Court;
   (b) in Northern Ireland, to the county court;
and an order so made may contain such provision as appears to the court to be appropriate for
delaying the coming into force of the order pending the making and determination of any appeal
(including any application under section 111 of the M4. Magistrates' Courts Act 1980 or Article
146 of the M5. Magistrates' Courts (Northern Ireland) Order 1981 (statement of case)).
Amendments (Textual)
F27. Words in s. 33. (1) substituted (1.10.2015) by Consumer Rights Act 2015 (c. 15), s. 100. (5),
Sch. 6 para. 44; S.I. 2015/1630, art. 3. (i) (with art. 8)

F28. Words in s. 33. (2)(a)(i) repealed (26.5.2008) by The Consumer Protection from Unfair Trading Regulations 2008 (S.I. 2008/1277), reg. 30. (3), Sch. 4 Pt. 1 (with reg. 28. (2)(3), Sch. 3 para. 6)

F29. Words in s. 33. (3)(a)(i) repealed (26.5.2008) by The Consumer Protection from Unfair Trading Regulations 2008 (S.I. 2008/1277), reg. 30. (3), Sch. 4 Pt. 1 (with reg. 28. (2)(3), Sch. 3 para. 6)

Modifications etc. (not altering text)
C42. S. 33 applied (with modifications) (1.1.1993) by S.I. 1992/3073, reg. 28, Sch. 6 para. 3. (c)
S. 33 applied (with modifications) (1.7.1997) by S.I. 1997/831, reg. 19. (1)-(4), Sch. 15 para. 2. (b) (with Sch. 15 para. 7)
Ss. 28-35 applied (with modifications) (31.5.1998) by S.I. 1998/1165, reg. 13. (2)(a) (which said S.I. was revoked (25.8.2003) by S.I. 2003/1941, reg. 1. (2))
Ss. 28-35 applied (with modifications) (26.4.1999) by S.I. 1999/1053, reg. 16. (3)(a)
Ss. 28-35 applied (with modifications) (29.11.1999) by S.I. 1999/2001, reg. 24, Sch. 8 para. 2. (c)
Ss. 28-35 applied (with modifications) (8.4.2000) by S.I. 2000/730, reg. 18. (1), Sch. 9 para. 1. (2)
Ss. 28-35 applied (with modifications) (15.5.2002) by S.I. 2002/1144, regs. 2. (2), 16. (1)-(3), Sch. 10 paras. 1, 3
Ss. 28-35 applied (with modifications) (25.8.2003) by S.I. 2003/1941, reg. 8, Sch. IV para. 2. (a)
C43. S. 33 applied (in part) (E.W.S) (28.11.2003 for certain purposes, 15.7.2004 for certain further purposes and otherwise prosp.) by Fireworks Act 2003 (c. 22), ss. 12. (2)(d), 18 (with s. 2. (8)); S.I. 2003/3084, art. 2, Sch.; S.I. 2004/1831, art. 2, Sch.
C44. S. 33 applied (with modifications) (17.8.2015) by The Pyrotechnic Articles (Safety) Regulations 2015 (S.I. 2015/1553), reg. 1, Sch. 7 paras. 1. (j), 2
C45. S. 33 applied (with modifications) (8.12.2016) by The Electrical Equipment (Safety) Regulations 2016 (S.I. 2016/1101), reg. 1, Sch. 3 paras. 1, 2 (with reg. 3)
C46. S. 33 applied (with modifications) (8.12.2016) by The Electromagnetic Compatibility Regulations 2016 (S.I. 2016/1091), reg. 1, Sch. 7 paras. 1, 2 (with regs. 74, 75. (5))
C47. S. 33 applied (with modifications) (8.12.2016) by The Simple Pressure Vessels (Safety) Regulations 2016 (S.I. 2016/1092), reg. 1, Sch. 5 paras. 1. (j), 2 (with reg. 3)
C48. S. 33 applied (with modifications) (8.12.2016) by The Pressure Equipment (Safety) Regulations 2016 (S.I. 2016/1105), reg. 1, Sch. 7 paras. 1. (j), 2 (with reg. 88)
C49. S. 33 applied (with modifications) (8.12.2016) by The Lifts Regulations 2016 (S.I. 2016/1093), reg. 1, Sch. 7 paras. 1. (i), 2 (with regs. 3-5)
C50. S. 33 applied (with modifications) (3.8.2017) by The Recreational Craft Regulations 2017 (S.I. 2017/737), reg. 1, Sch. 13 paras. 1. (j), 2 (with reg. 89)
C51. S. 33 applied (with modifications) (26.12.2017) by The Radio Equipment Regulations 2017 (S.I. 2017/1206), reg. 1, Sch. 10 paras. 1, 2 (with regs. 3-5, 77)
Marginal Citations
M41980 c. 43.
M5. S.I. 1981/1675 (N.I. 26).

34 Compensation for seizure and detention.

(1) Where an officer of an enforcement authority exercises any power under section [F3029. (4)] above to seize and detain goods, the enforcement authority shall be liable to pay compensation to any person having an interest in the goods in respect of any loss or damage caused by reason of the exercise of the power if—

(a) there has been no contravention in relation to the goods of any safety provision F31. . . ; and
(b) the exercise of the power is not attributable to any neglect or default by that person.

(2) Any disputed question as to the right to or the amount of any compensation payable under this section shall be determined by arbitration or, in Scotland, by a single arbiter appointed, failing agreement between the parties, by the sheriff.

Amendments (Textual)

F30. Word in s. 34. (1) substituted (1.10.2015) by Consumer Rights Act 2015 (c. 15), s. 100. (5), Sch. 6 para. 45; S.I. 2015/1630, art. 3. (i) (with art. 8)

F31. Words in s. 34. (1)(a) repealed (26.5.2008) by The Consumer Protection from Unfair Trading Regulations 2008 (S.I. 2008/1277), reg. 30. (3), Sch. 4 Pt. 1 (with reg. 28. (2)(3), Sch. 3 para. 6)

Modifications etc. (not altering text)

C52. S. 34 applied (with modifications) (1.1.1993) by S.I. 1992/3073, reg. 28, Sch. 6 para. 3. (c).

S. 34 applied (with modifications) (1.7.1997) by S.I. 1997/831, reg. 19. (1)-(4), Sch. 15 para. 2. (b) (with Sch. 15 para. 7) Ss. 28-35 applied (with modifications) (31.5.1998) by S.I. 1998/1165, reg. 13. (2)(a) (which said S.I. was revoked (25.8.2003) by S.I. 2003/1941, reg. 1. (2)) Ss. 28-35 applied (with modifications) (26.4.1999) by S.I. 1999/1053, reg. 16. (3)(a) Ss. 28-35 applied (with modifications) (29.11.1999) by S.I. 1999/2001, reg. 24, Sch. 8 para. 2. (c)

Ss. 28-35 applied (with modifications) (8.4.2000) by S.I. 2000/730, reg. 18. (1), Sch. 9 para. 1. (2)

Ss. 28-35 applied (with modifications) (15.5.2002) by S.I. 2002/1144, regs. 2. (2), 16. (1)-(3), Sch. 10 paras. 1, 3

Ss. 28-35 applied (with modifications) (25.8.2003) by S.I. 2003/1941, reg 8, Sch. 4 para. 2. (a)

C53. S. 34 applied (E.W.S) (28.11.2003 for certain purposes, 15.7.2004 for certain further purposes and otherwise prosp.) by Fireworks Act 2003 (c. 22), ss. 12. (2)(e), 18 (with s. 2. (8)); S.I. 2003/3084, art. 2, Sch.; S.I. 2004/1831, art. 2, Sch.

C54. S. 34 applied (1.4.2003) by 2001 c. 16, ss. 70, 138. (2), Sch. 2 Pt. 1 para. 8; S.I. 2003/708, art. 2. (k)

C55. S. 34 applied (with modifications) (17.8.2015) by The Pyrotechnic Articles (Safety) Regulations 2015 (S.I. 2015/1553), reg. 1, Sch. 7 paras. 1. (k), 2

C56. S. 34 applied (with modifications) (8.12.2016) by The Electromagnetic Compatibility Regulations 2016 (S.I. 2016/1091), reg. 1, Sch. 7 paras. 1, 2 (with regs. 74, 75. (5))

C57. S. 34 applied (with modifications) (8.12.2016) by The Simple Pressure Vessels (Safety) Regulations 2016 (S.I. 2016/1092), reg. 1, Sch. 5 paras. 1. (k), 2 (with reg. 3)

C58. S. 34 applied (with modifications) (8.12.2016) by The Pressure Equipment (Safety) Regulations 2016 (S.I. 2016/1105), reg. 1, Sch. 7 paras. 1. (k), 2 (with reg. 88)

C59. S. 34 applied (with modifications) (8.12.2016) by The Lifts Regulations 2016 (S.I. 2016/1093), reg. 1, Sch. 7 paras. 1. (j), 2 (with regs. 3-5)

C60. S. 34 applied (with modifications) (8.12.2016) by The Electrical Equipment (Safety) Regulations 2016 (S.I. 2016/1101), reg. 1, Sch. 3 paras. 1, 2 (with reg. 3)

C61. S. 34 applied (with modifications) (3.8.2017) by The Recreational Craft Regulations 2017 (S.I. 2017/737), reg. 1, Sch. 13 paras. 1. (k), 2 (with reg. 89)

C62. S. 34 applied (with modifications) (26.12.2017) by The Radio Equipment Regulations 2017 (S.I. 2017/1206), reg. 1, Sch. 10 paras. 1, 2 (with regs. 3-5, 77)

35 Recovery of expenses of enforcement.

(1) This section shall apply where a court—
  (a) convicts a person of an offence in respect of a contravention in relation to any goods of any safety provision F32. . . ; or
  (b) makes an order under section 16 or 17 above for the forfeiture of any goods.

(2) The court may (in addition to any other order it may make as to costs or expenses) order the person convicted or, as the case may be, any person having an interest in the goods to reimburse an enforcement authority for any expenditure which has been or may be incurred by that authority—
  (a) in connection with any seizure or detention of the goods by or on behalf of the authority; or
  (b) in connection with any compliance by the authority with directions given by the court for the purposes of any order for the forfeiture of the goods.

Amendments (Textual)

F32. Words in s. 35. (1)(a) repealed (26.5.2008) by The Consumer Protection from Unfair Trading Regulations 2008 (S.I. 2008/1277), reg. 30. (3), Sch. 4 Pt. 1 (with reg. 28. (2)(3), Sch. 3 para. 6)
Modifications etc. (not altering text)
C63. S. 35 applied (with modifications) (1.1.1993) by S.I. 1992/3073, reg. 28, Sch. 6 para. 3. (c)
S. 35 applied (with modifications) (1.7.1997) by S.I. 1997/831, reg. 19. (1)-(4), Sch. 15 para. 2. (b) (with Sch. 15 para. 7)
Ss. 28-35 applied (with modifications) (31.5.1998) by S.I. 1998/1165, reg. 13. (2)(a) (which said S.I. was revoked (25.8.2003) by S.I. 2003/1941, reg. 1. (2))
Ss. 28-35 applied (with modifications) (26.4.1999) by S.I. 1999/1053, reg. 16. (3)(a)
Ss. 28-35 applied (with modifications) (29.11.1999) by S.I. 1999/2001, reg. 24, Sch. 8 para. 2. (c)
Ss. 28-35 applied (with modifications) (8.4.2000) by S.I. 2000/730, reg. 18. (1), Sch. 9 para. 1. (2)
Ss. 28-35 applied (with modifications) (15.5.2002) by S.I. 2002/1144, regs. 2. (2), 16. (1)-(3), Sch. 10 paras. 1, 3
Ss. 28-35 applied (with modifications) (25.8.2003) by S.I. 2003/1941, reg. 8, Sch. IV para. 2. (a)
C64. S. 35 applied (in part) (E.W.S) (28.11.2003 for certain purposes, 15.7.2004 for certain further purposes and otherwise prosp.) by Fireworks Act 2003 (c. 22), ss. 12. (2)(f), 18 (with s. 2. (8)); S.I. 2003/3084, art. 2, Sch.; S.I. 2004/1831, art. 2, Sch.
C65. S. 35 applied (with modifications) (17.8.2015) by The Pyrotechnic Articles (Safety) Regulations 2015 (S.I. 2015/1553), reg. 1, Sch. 7 paras. 1. (l), 2
C66. S. 35 applied (with modifications) (8.12.2016) by The Lifts Regulations 2016 (S.I. 2016/1093), reg. 1, Sch. 7 paras. 1. (k), 2 (with regs. 3-5)
C67. S. 35 applied (with modifications) (8.12.2016) by The Pressure Equipment (Safety) Regulations 2016 (S.I. 2016/1105), reg. 1, Sch. 7 paras. 1. (l), 2 (with reg. 88)
C68. S. 35 applied (with modifications) (8.12.2016) by The Electromagnetic Compatibility Regulations 2016 (S.I. 2016/1091), reg. 1, Sch. 7 paras. 1, 2 (with regs. 74, 75. (5))
C69. S. 35 applied (with modifications) (8.12.2016) by The Simple Pressure Vessels (Safety) Regulations 2016 (S.I. 2016/1092), reg. 1, Sch. 5 paras. 1. (l), 2 (with reg. 3)
C70. S. 35 applied (with modifications) (8.12.2016) by The Electrical Equipment (Safety) Regulations 2016 (S.I. 2016/1101), reg. 1, Sch. 3 paras. 1, 2 (with reg. 3)
C71. S. 35 applied (with modifications) (3.8.2017) by The Recreational Craft Regulations 2017 (S.I. 2017/737), reg. 1, Sch. 13 paras. 1. (l), 2 (with reg. 89)
C72. S. 35 applied (with modifications) (26.12.2017) by The Radio Equipment Regulations 2017 (S.I. 2017/1206), reg. 1, Sch. 10 paras. 1, 2 (with regs. 3-5, 77)

Part V Miscellaneous and Supplemental

Part V Miscellaneous and Supplemental

Modifications etc. (not altering text)
C1. Pt. V applied in part (with modifications) (20.5.2016) by The Tobacco and Related Products Regulations 2016 (S.I. 2016/507), regs. 1. (2), 53. (3)

36 Amendments of Part I of the Health and Safety at Work etc. Act 1974.

Part I of the M1. Health and Safety at Work etc. Act 1974 (which includes provision with respect to the safety of certain articles and substances) shall have effect with the amendments specified in Schedule 3 to this Act; and, accordingly, the general purposes of that Part of that Act shall include the purpose of protecting persons from the risks protection from which would not be afforded by virtue of that Part but for those amendments.

Marginal Citations
M11974 c. 37.

37[F1. Power of Commissioners for Revenue and Customs to disclose information]

(1) If they think it appropriate to do so for the purpose of facilitating the exercise by any person to whom subsection (2) below applies of any functions conferred on that person by or under Part II of this Act, or by or under Part IV of this Act in its application for the purposes of the safety provisions, [F2the Commissioners for Her Majesty's Revenue and Customs] may authorise the disclosure to that person of any information obtained [F3or held] for the purposes of the exercise [F4by Her Majesty's Revenue and Customs] of their functions in relation to imported goods.
(2) This subsection applies to an enforcement authority and to any officer of an enforcement authority.
(3) A disclosure of information made to any person under subsection (1) above shall be made in such manner as may be directed by [F5the Commissioners for Her Majesty's Revenue and Customs] and may be made through such persons acting on behalf of that person as may be so directed.
(4) Information may be disclosed to a person under subsection (1) above whether or not the disclosure of the information has been requested by or on behalf of that person.

Amendments (Textual)
F1. S. 37 heading substituted (18.4.2005) by Commissioners for Revenue and Customs Act 2005 (c. 11), ss. 50, 53. (1), Sch. 4 para. 36. (4); S.I. 2005/1126, art. 2. (2)(h)
F2. Words in s. 37. (1) substituted (18.4.2005) by Commissioners for Revenue and Customs Act 2005 (c. 11), ss. 50, 53. (1), Sch. 4 para. 36. (2)(a); S.I. 2005/1126, art. {2. (2)(h)}
F3. Words in s. 37. (1) inserted (18.4.2005) by Commissioners for Revenue and Customs Act 2005 (c. 11), ss. 50, 53. (1), Sch. 4 para. 36. (2)(b); S.I. 2005/1126, art. {2. (2)(h)}
F4. Words in s. 37. (1) substituted (18.4.2005) by Commissioners for Revenue and Customs Act 2005 (c. 11), ss. 50, 53. (1), Sch. 4 para. 36. (2)(c); S.I. 2005/1126, art. {2. (2)(h)}
F5. Words in s. 37. (3) substituted (18.4.2005) by Commissioners for Revenue and Customs Act 2005 (c. 11), ss. 50, 53. (1), Sch. 4 para. 36. (3); S.I. 2005/1126, art. {2. (2)(h)}

Modifications etc. (not altering text)
C2. S. 37 applied (E.W.S) (28.11.2003 for certain purposes, 15.7.2004 for certain further purposes and otherwise prosp.) by Fireworks Act 2003 (c. 22), ss. 12. (2)(g), 18 (with s. 2. (8)); S.I. 2003/3084, art. 2, Sch.; S.I. 2004/1831, art. 2, Sch.
C3. S. 37 applied (with modifications) (1.1.1993) by S.I. 1992/3073, reg. 28, Sch. 6 para. 3. (c).
S. 37 applied (3.10.1994) by S.I. 1994/2328. reg. 11. (c)(i)
S. 37 applied (with modifications) (1.7.1997) by S.I. 1997/831, reg. 19. (1)-(4), Sch. 15 para. 2. (b) (with Sch. 15 para. 7)
S. 37 applied (with modifications) (31.5.1998) by S.I. 1998/1165, reg. 13. (2)(a) (which said S.I. was revoked (25.8.2003) by S.I. 2003/1941, reg. 1. (2))
S. 37 applied (with modifications) (26.4.1999) by S.I. 1999/1053, reg. 16. (3)(a)
S. 37 applied (with modifications) (29.11.1999) by S.I. 1999/2001, reg. 24, Sch. 8 para. 2. (c)
S. 37 applied (with modifications) (8.4.2000) by S.I. 2000/730, reg. 18. (1), Sch. 9 para. 1. (2)
S. 37 applied (with modifications) (15.5.2002) by S.I. 2002/1144, regs. 2. (2), 16. (1)-(3), Sch. 10 paras. 1, 3
S. 37 applied (with modifications) (25.8.2003) by S.I. 2003/1941, reg. 8, Sch. IV para. 2. (a)
C4. S. 37 applied (with modifications) (17.8.2015) by The Pyrotechnic Articles (Safety) Regulations 2015 (S.I. 2015/1553), reg. 1, Sch. 7 paras. 1. (m), 2
C5. S. 37 applied (with modifications) (1.10.2015) by The Packaging (Essential Requirements) Regulations 2015 (S.I. 2015/1640), reg. 1, Sch. 4 para. 1. (1)(a) (with reg. 3. (5))
C6. S. 37 applied (with modifications) (8.12.2016) by The Lifts Regulations 2016 (S.I.

2016/1093), reg. 1, Sch. 7 paras. 1. (l), 2 (with regs. 3-5)
C7. S. 37 applied (with modifications) (8.12.2016) by The Electromagnetic Compatibility Regulations 2016 (S.I. 2016/1091), reg. 1, Sch. 7 paras. 1, 2 (with regs. 74, 75. (5))
C8. S. 37 applied (with modifications) (8.12.2016) by The Electrical Equipment (Safety) Regulations 2016 (S.I. 2016/1101), reg. 1, Sch. 3 paras. 1, 2 (with reg. 3)
C9. S. 37 applied (with modifications) (8.12.2016) by The Pressure Equipment (Safety) Regulations 2016 (S.I. 2016/1105), reg. 1, Sch. 7 paras. 1. (m), 2 (with reg. 88)
C10. S. 37 applied (with modifications) (8.12.2016) by The Simple Pressure Vessels (Safety) Regulations 2016 (S.I. 2016/1092), reg. 1, Sch. 5 paras. 1. (m), 2 (with reg. 3)
C11. S. 37 applied (with modifications) (3.8.2017) by The Recreational Craft Regulations 2017 (S.I. 2017/737), reg. 1, Sch. 13 paras. 1. (m), 2 (with reg. 89)
C12. S. 37 applied (with modifications) (26.12.2017) by The Radio Equipment Regulations 2017 (S.I. 2017/1206), reg. 1, Sch. 10 paras. 1, 2 (with regs. 3-5, 77)

38 Restrictions on disclosure of information.

F6. . . . .
Amendments (Textual)
F6. S. 38 repealed (20.6.2003) by 2002 c. 40, ss. 247. (g), 278. (2), 279, Sch. 26; S.I. 2003/1397, art. 2. (1), Sch. (with art. 10)

39 Defence of due diligence.

(1) Subject to the following provisions of this section, in proceedings against any person for an offence to which this section applies it shall be a defence for that person to show that he took all reasonable steps and exercised all due diligence to avoid committing the offence.
(2) Where in any proceedings against any person for such an offence the defence provided by subsection (1) above involves an allegation that the commission of the offence was due—
 (a) to the act or default of another; or
 (b) to reliance on information given by another,
that person shall not, without the leave of the court, be entitled to rely on the defence unless, not less than seven clear days before the hearing of the proceedings, he has served a notice under subsection (3) below on the person bringing the proceedings.
(3) A notice under this subsection shall give such information identifying or assisting in the identification of the person who committed the act or default or gave the information as is in the possession of the person serving the notice at the time he serves it.
(4) It is hereby declared that a person shall not be entitled to rely on the defence provided by subsection (1) above by reason of his reliance on information supplied by another, unless he shows that it was reasonable in all the circumstances for him to have relied on the information, having regard in particular—
 (a) to the steps which he took, and those which might reasonably have been taken, for the purpose of verifying the information; and
 (b) to whether he had any reason to disbelieve the information.
(5) This section shall apply to an offence under section F7. . . 12. (1), (2) or (3), 13. (4), [F8or 14. (6)] above.
Amendments (Textual)
F7. Word in s. 39. (5) omitted (1.10.2005) by virtue of The General Product Safety Regulations 2005 (S.I. 2005/1803), reg. 46. (6) (with regs. 42, 43)
F8. Words in s. 39. (5) substituted (26.5.2008) by The Consumer Protection from Unfair Trading Regulations 2008 (S.I. 2008/1277), reg. 30. (1), Sch. 2 para. 35 (with reg. 28. (2)(3))
Modifications etc. (not altering text)
C13. S. 39 applied by S.I. 1991/199, reg. 8. (2)(b).

C14. S. 39 applied (with modifications) (1.1.1993) by S.I. 1992/3073, reg. 28, Sch. 6 para. 3. (c)(d).
S. 39 applied (with modifications) (1.7.1997) by S.I. 1997/831, reg. 19. (1)-(4), Sch. 15 para. 2. (c) (with Sch. 15 para. 7)
C15. S. 39 applied (18.5.1992) by S.I. 1992/737, reg. 9. (3)(b)
S. 39 applied (20.2.1995) by S.I. 1994/3248, reg. 8. (2)(b)
S. 39 applied (with modifications) (31.5.1998) by S.I. 1998/1165, reg. 13. (2)(b) (which said S.I. was revoked (25.8.2003) by S.I. 2003/1941, reg. 1. (2))
S. 39 applied (with modifications) (26.4.1999) by S.I. 1999/1053, reg. 16. (3)(b)
S. 39 applied (with modifications) (8.4.2000) by S.I. 2000/730, reg. 18. (1), Sch. 9 para. 1. (3)
S. 39 applied (25.8.2003) by S.I. 2003/1941, reg. 8, Sch. IV para. 2. (b)
S. 39 applied (with modifications) (E.W.S) (28.11.2003 for certain purposes and 15.7.2004 for certain further purposes and otherwise prosp.) by Fireworks Act 2003 (c. 22), ss. 11. (7), 18 (with s. 2. (8)); S.I. 2003/3084, art. 2, Sch.; S.I 2004/1831, {art. 2}, Sch.
C16. S. 39 applied (1.10.2015) by The Packaging (Essential Requirements) Regulations 2015 (S.I. 2015/1640), reg. 1, Sch. 4 para. 1. (1)(b) (with reg. 3. (5))

40 Liability of persons other than principal offender.

(1) Where the commission by any person of an offence to which section 39 above applies is due to an act or default committed by some other person in the course of any business of his, the other person shall be guilty of the offence and may be proceeded against and punished by virtue of this subsection whether or not proceedings are taken against the first-mentioned person.
(2) Where a body corporate is guilty of an offence under this Act (including where it is so guilty by virtue of subsection (1) above) in respect of any act or default which is shown to have been committed with the consent or connivance of, or to be attributable to any neglect on the part of, any director, manager, secretary or other similar officer of the body corporate or any person who was purporting to act in any such capacity he, as well as the body corporate, shall be guilty of that offence and shall be liable to be proceeded against and punished accordingly.
(3) Where the affairs of a body corporate are managed by its members, subsection (2) above shall apply in relation to the acts and defaults of a member in connection with his functions of management as if he were a director of the body corporate.
Modifications etc. (not altering text)
C17. S. 40 applied (with modifications) (1.1.1993) by S.I. 1992/3073, reg. 28, Sch. 6 para. 3. (c)(d).
S. 40 applied (with modifications) (1.7.1997) by S.I. 1997/831, reg. 19. (1)-(4), Sch. 15 para. 2. (c) (with Sch. 15 para. 7)
S. 40 applied (with modifications) (31.5.1998) by S.I. 1998/1165, reg. 13. (2)(b) (which said S.I. was revoked (25.8.2003) by S.I. 2003/1941, reg. 1. (2))
S. 40 applied (with modifications) (26.4.1999) by S.I. 1999/1053, reg. 16. (3)(b)
S. 40 applied (with modifications) (8.4.2000) by S.I. 2000/730, reg. 18. (1), Sch. 9 para. 1. (3)
S. 40 applied (25.8.2003) by S.I. 2003/1941, reg. 8, Sch. IV para. 2. (b)
C18. S. 40 applied (1.10.2015) by The Packaging (Essential Requirements) Regulations 2015 (S.I. 2015/1640), reg. 1, Sch. 4 para. 1. (1)(b) (with reg. 3. (5))
C19. S. 40. (1)(2)(3) applied by S.I. 1991/199, reg. 8. (2)(c)
C20. S. 40. (1)(2)(3) applied (18.5.1992) by S.I. 1992/737, reg. 9. (3)(c)
S. 40. (1) applied (20.2.1995) by S.I. 1994/3248, reg. 8. (2)(c);
S. 40. (1) modified (E.W.S) (28.11.2003 for certain purposes and otherwise prosp.) by Fireworks Act 2003 (c. 22), ss. 11. (7), 18 (with s. 2. (8)); S.I. 2003/3084, art. 2, Sch.
C21. S. 40. (1)(2)(3) applied by S.I. 1991/199, reg. 8. (2)(c)
S. 40. (2)(3) applied (E.W.S) (28.11.2003 for certain purposes and otherwise prosp.) by Fireworks Act 2003 (c. 22), ss. 11. (9), 18 (with s. 2. (8)); S.I. 2003/3084, art. 2, Sch.

41 Civil proceedings.

(1) An obligation imposed by safety regulations shall be a duty owed to any person who may be affected by a contravention of the obligation and, subject to any provision to the contrary in the regulations and to the defences and other incidents applying to actions for breach of statutory duty, a contravention of any such obligation shall be actionable accordingly.

(2) This Act shall not be construed as conferring any other right of action in civil proceedings, apart from the right conferred by virtue of Part I of this Act, in respect of any loss or damage suffered in consequence of a contravention of a safety provision F9. . . .

(3) Subject to any provision to the contrary in the agreement itself, an agreement shall not be void or unenforceable by reason only of a contravention of a safety provision F10. . . .

(4) Liability by virtue of subsection (1) above shall not be limited or excluded by any contract term, by any notice or (subject to the power contained in subsection (1) above to limit or exclude it in safety regulations) by any other provision.

(5) Nothing in subsection (1) above shall prejudice the operation of section 12 of the M2. Nuclear Installations Act 1965 (rights to compensation for certain breaches of duties confined to rights under that Act).

(6) In this section "damage" includes personal injury and death.

Amendments (Textual)
F9. Words in s. 41. (2) repealed (26.5.2008) by The Consumer Protection from Unfair Trading Regulations 2008 (S.I. 2008/1277), reg. 30. (3), Sch. 4 Pt. 1 (with reg. 28. (2)(3), Sch. 3 para. 6)
F10. Words in s. 41. (3) repealed (26.5.2008) by The Consumer Protection from Unfair Trading Regulations 2008 (S.I. 2008/1277), reg. 30. (3), Sch. 4 Pt. 1 (with reg. 28. (2)(3), Sch. 3 para. 6)
Modifications etc. (not altering text)
C22. S. 41 applied (E.W.S) (28.11.2003 for certain purposes, 15.7.2004 for certain further purposes and otherwise prosp.) by Fireworks Act 2003 (c. 22), ss. 12. (2)(h), 18 (with s. 2. (8)); S.I. 2003/3084, art. 2, Sch.; S.I. 2004/1831, art. 2, Sch.
Marginal Citations
M21965 c.57.

42 Reports etc.

(1) It shall be the duty of the Secretary of State at least once in every five years to lay before each House of Parliament a report on the exercise during the period to which the report relates of the functions which under Part II of this Act, or under Part IV of this Act in its application for the purposes of the safety provisions, are exercisable by the Secretary of State, weights and measures authorities, district councils in Northern Ireland and persons on whom functions are conferred by regulations made under section 27. (2) above.

(2) The Secretary of State may from time to time prepare and lay before each House of Parliament such other reports on the exercise of those functions as he considers appropriate.

(3) Every weights and measures authority, every district council in Northern Ireland and every person on whom functions are conferred by regulations under subsection (2) of section 27 above shall, whenever the Secretary of State so directs, make a report to the Secretary of State on the exercise of the functions exercisable by that authority or council under that section or by that person by virtue of any such regulations.

(4) A report under subsection (3) above shall be in such form and shall contain such particulars as are specified in the direction of the Secretary of State.

(5) The first report under subsection (1) above shall be laid before each House of Parliament not more than five years after the laying of the last report under section 8. (2) of the M3. Consumer Safety Act 1978.

Modifications etc. (not altering text)

C23. S. 42 applied (with modifications) (3.8.2017) by The Recreational Craft Regulations 2017 (S.I. 2017/737), reg. 1, Sch. 13 paras. 1. (n), 2 (with reg. 89)
C24. S. 42. (3)(4) applied (3.10.1994) by S.I. 1994/2328, reg. 11. (c)(i)
Marginal Citations
M31978 c. 38.

43 Financial provisions.

(1) There shall be paid out of money provided by Parliament—
    (a) any expenses incurred or compensation payable by a Minister of the Crown or Government department in consequence of any provision of this Act; and
    (b) any increase attributable to this Act in the sums payable out of money so provided under any other Act.
(2) Any sums received by a Minister of the Crown or Government department by virtue of this Act shall be paid into the Consolidated Fund.

44 Service of documents etc.

(1) Any document required or authorised by virtue of this Act to be served on a person may be so served—
    (a) by delivering it to him or by leaving it at his proper address or by sending it by post to him at that address; or
    (b) if the person is a body corporate, by serving it in accordance with paragraph (a) above on the secretary or clerk of that body; or
    (c) if the person is a partnership, by serving it in accordance with that paragraph on a partner or on a person having control or management of the partnership business.
(2) For the purposes of subsection (1) above, and for the purposes of section 7 of the M4. Interpretation Act 1978 (which relates to the service of documents by post) in its application to that subsection, the proper address of any person on whom a document is to be served by virtue of this Act shall be his last known address except that—
    (a) in the case of service on a body corporate or its secretary or clerk, it shall be the address of the registered or principal office of the body corporate;
    (b) in the case of service on a partnership or a partner or a person having the control or management of a partnership business, it shall be the principal office of the partnership;
and for the purposes of this subsection the principal office of a company registered outside the United Kingdom or of a partnership carrying on business outside the United Kingdom is its principal office within the United Kingdom.
(3) The Secretary of State may by regulations make provision for the manner in which any information is to be given to any person under any provision of Part IV of this Act.
(4) Without prejudice to the generality of subsection (3) above regulations made by the Secretary of State may prescribe the person, or manner of determining the person, who is to be treated for the purposes of section F11... 30 above as the person from whom any goods were F12... seized where the goods were F12... seized from a vending machine.
(5) The power to make regulations under subsection (3) or (4) above shall be exercisable by statutory instrument subject to annulment in pursuance of a resolution of either House of Parliament and shall include power—
    (a) to make different provision for different cases; and
    (b) to make such supplemental, consequential and transitional provision as the Secretary of State considers appropriate.
Amendments (Textual)
F11. Words in s. 44. (4) omitted (1.10.2015) by virtue of Consumer Rights Act 2015 (c. 15), s. 100. (5), Sch. 6 para. 46. (a); S.I. 2015/1630, art. 3. (i) (with art. 8)

F12. Words in s. 44. (4) omitted (1.10.2015) by virtue of Consumer Rights Act 2015 (c. 15), s. 100. (5), Sch. 6 para. 46. (b); S.I. 2015/1630, art. 3. (i) (with art. 8)

Modifications etc. (not altering text)

C25. S. 44 applied (with modifications) (1.1.1993) by S.I. 1992/3073, reg. 28, Sch. 6 para. 3. (c)
S. 44 applied (with modifications) (1.7.1997) by S.I. 1997/831, reg. 19. (1)-(4), Sch. 15 para. 2. (b) (with Sch. 15 para. 7)
S. 44 applied (with modifications) (31.5.1998) by S.I. 1998/1165, reg. 13. (2)(a) (which said S.I. was revoked (25.8.2003) by S.I. 2003/1941, reg. 1. (2))
S. 44 applied (with modifications) (26.4.1999) by S.I. 1999/1053, reg. 16. (3)(a)
S. 44 applied (with modifications) (29.11.1999) by S.I. 1999/2001, reg. 24, Sch. 8 para. 2. (c)
S. 44 applied (with modifications) (8.4.2000) by S.I. 2000/730, reg. 18. (1), Sch. 9 para. 1. (2)
S. 44 applied (with modifications) (15.5.2002) by S.I. 2002/1144, regs. 2. (2), 16. (1)-(3), Sch. 10 paras. 1, 3
S. 44 applied (with modifications) (25.8.2003) by S.I. 2003/1941, reg. 8, Sch. IV para. 2. (a)
S. 44 applied (E.W.S) (28.11.2003 for certain purposes, 15.7.2004 for certain further purposes and otherwise prosp.) by Fireworks Act 2003 (c. 22), ss. 12. (2)(i), 18 (with s. 2. (8)); S.I. 2003/3084, art. 2, Sch.; S.I. 2004/1831, art. 2, Sch.

C26. S. 44 applied (with modifications) (1.10.2015) by The Packaging (Essential Requirements) Regulations 2015 (S.I. 2015/1640), reg. 1, Sch. 4 para. 1. (1)(a) (with reg. 3. (5))

Marginal Citations

M41978 c. 30.

45 Interpretation.

(1) In this Act, except in so far as the context otherwise requires—

"aircraft" includes gliders, balloons and hovercraft;

"business" includes a trade or profession and the activities of a professional or trade association or of a local authority or other public authority;

"conditional sale agreement", "credit—sale agreement" and "hire-purchase agreement" have the same meanings as in the M5. Consumer Credit Act 1974 but as if in the definitions in that Act "goods" had the same meaning as in this Act;

"contravention" includes a failure to comply and cognate expressions shall be construed accordingly;

"enforcement authority" means the Secretary of State, any other Minister of the Crown in charge of a Government department, any such department and any authority, council or other person on whom functions under this Act are conferred by or under section 27 above;

"gas" has the same meaning as in Part I of the M6. Gas Act 1986;

"goods" includes substances, growing crops and things comprised in land by virtue of being attached to it and any ship, aircraft or vehicle;

"information" includes accounts, estimates and returns;

"magistrates' court", in relation to Northern Ireland, means a court of summary jurisdiction; F13. . .

"modifications" includes additions, alterations and omissions, and cognate expressions shall be construed accordingly;

"motor vehicle" has the same meaning as in [F14the Road Traffic Act 1988];

"notice" means a notice in writing;

"notice to warn" means a notice under section 13. (1)(b) above;

"officer", in relation to an enforcement authority, means a person authorised in writing to assist the authority in carrying out its functions under or for the purposes of the enforcement of any of the safety provisions or of any of the provisions made by or under Part III of this Act;

"personal injury" includes any disease and any other impairment of a person's physical or mental condition;

"premises" includes any place and any ship, aircraft or vehicle;
"prohibition notice" means a notice under section 13. (1)(a) above;
"records" includes any books or documents and any records in non-documentary form;
"safety provision" means F15. . . any provision of safety regulations, a prohibition notice or a suspension notice;
"safety regulations" means regulations under section 11 above;
"ship" includes any boat and any other description of vessel used in navigation;
"subordinate legislation" has the same meaning as in the M7. Interpretation Act 1978;
"substance" means any natural or artificial substance, whether in solid, liquid or gaseous form or in the form of a vapour, and includes substances that are comprised in or mixed with other goods;
"supply" and cognate expressions shall be construed in accordance with section 46 below;
"suspension notice" means a notice under section 14 above.

(2) Except in so far as the context otherwise requires, references in this Act to a contravention of a safety provision shall, in relation to any goods, include references to anything which would constitute such a contravention if the goods were supplied to any person.

(3) References in this Act to any goods in relation to which any safety provision has been or may have been contravened shall include references to any goods which it is not reasonably practicable to separate from any such goods.

F16. (4). . . . .

(5) In Scotland, any reference in this Act to things comprised in land by virtue of being attached to it is a reference to moveables which have become heritable by accession to heritable property.

Amendments (Textual)
F13. Definitions in s. 45. (1) repealed (31.10.1994) by 1994 c. 26, s. 106. (2), Sch. 5; S.I. 1994/2550, art. 2
F14. Words substituted by Road Traffic (Consequential Provisions) Act 1988 (c. 54, SIF 107:1), s. 4, Sch. 3 para. 35
F15. Words in definition of "safety provision" in s. 45. (1) omitted (1.10.2005) by virtue of The General Product Safety Regulations 2005 (S.I. 2005/1803), reg. 46. (7) (with regs. 42, 43)
F16. S. 45. (4) repealed (31.10.1994) by 1994 c. 26, s. 106. (2), Sch. 5; S.I. 1994/2550, art. 2

Modifications etc. (not altering text)
C27. S. 45 applied (with modifications) (17.8.2015) by The Pyrotechnic Articles (Safety) Regulations 2015 (S.I. 2015/1553), reg. 1, Sch. 7 paras. 1. (n), 2
C28. S. 45 applied (with modifications) (8.12.2016) by The Lifts Regulations 2016 (S.I. 2016/1093), reg. 1, Sch. 7 paras. 1. (m), 2 (with regs. 3-5)
C29. S. 45 applied (with modifications) (8.12.2016) by The Electrical Equipment (Safety) Regulations 2016 (S.I. 2016/1101), reg. 1, Sch. 3 paras. 1, 2 (with reg. 3)
C30. S. 45 applied (with modifications) (8.12.2016) by The Simple Pressure Vessels (Safety) Regulations 2016 (S.I. 2016/1092), reg. 1, Sch. 5 paras. 1. (n), 2 (with reg. 3)
C31. S. 45 applied (with modifications) (8.12.2016) by The Electromagnetic Compatibility Regulations 2016 (S.I. 2016/1091), reg. 1, Sch. 7 paras. 1, 2 (with regs. 74, 75. (5))
C32. S. 45 applied (with modifications) (8.12.2016) by The Pressure Equipment (Safety) Regulations 2016 (S.I. 2016/1105), reg. 1, Sch. 7 paras. 1. (n), 2 (with reg. 88)
C33. S. 45 applied (with modifications) (3.8.2017) by The Recreational Craft Regulations 2017 (S.I. 2017/737), reg. 1, Sch. 13 paras. 1. (o), 2 (with reg. 89)
C34. S. 45 applied (with modifications) (26.12.2017) by The Radio Equipment Regulations 2017 (S.I. 2017/1206), reg. 1, Sch. 10 paras. 1, 2 (with regs. 3-5, 77)
C35. By the Low Voltage Electrical Equipment (Safety) Regulations 1989, S.I. 1989/728, reg. 14. (1) it is provided that those Regulations shall be treated for all purposes as if they were safety regulations within the meaning of section 45. (1) of this Act

Marginal Citations
M51974 c. 39.
M61986 c. 44.
M71978 c. 30.

46 Meaning of "supply"

(1) Subject to the following provisions of this section, references in this Act to supplying goods shall be construed as references to doing any of the following, whether as principal or agent, that is to say—
   (a) selling, hiring out or lending the goods;
   (b) entering into a hire-purchase agreement to furnish the goods;
   (c) the performance of any contract for work and materials to furnish the goods;
   (d) providing the goods in exchange for any consideration F17. . . other than money;
   (e) providing the goods in or in connection with the performance of any statutory function; or
   (f) giving the goods as a prize or otherwise making a gift of the goods;
and, in relation to gas or water, those references shall be construed as including references to providing the service by which the gas or water is made available for use.

(2) For the purposes of any reference in this Act to supplying goods, where a person ("the ostensible supplier") supplies goods to another person ("the customer") under a hire-purchase agreement, conditional sale agreement or credit-sale agreement or under an agreement for the hiring of goods (other than a hire-purchase agreement) and the ostensible supplier—
   (a) carries on the business of financing the provision of goods for others by means of such agreements; and
   (b) in the course of that business acquired his interest in the goods supplied to the customer as a means of financing the provision of them for the customer by a further person ("the effective supplier"),
the effective supplier and not the ostensible supplier shall be treated as supplying the goods to the customer.

(3) Subject to subsection (4) below, the performance of any contract by the erection of any building or structure on any land or by the carrying out of any other building works shall be treated for the purposes of this Act as a supply of goods in so far as, but only in so far as, it involves the provision of any goods to any person by means of their incorporation into the building, structure or works.

(4) Except for the purposes of, and in relation to, notices to warn F18. . . , references in this Act to supplying goods shall not include references to supplying goods comprised in land where the supply is effected by the creation or disposal of an interest in the land.

(5) Except in Part I of this Act references in this Act to a person's supplying goods shall be confined to references to that person's supplying goods in the course of a business of his, but for the purposes of this subsection it shall be immaterial whether the business is a business of dealing in the goods.

(6) For the purposes of subsection (5) above goods shall not be treated as supplied in the course of a business if they are supplied, in pursuance of an obligation arising under or in connection with the insurance of the goods, to the person with whom they were insured.

(7) Except for the purposes of, and in relation to, prohibition notices or suspension notices, references in [F19. Part 2 or Part 4] of this Act to supplying goods shall not include—
   (a) references to supplying goods where the person supplied carries on a business of buying goods of the same description as those goods and repairing or reconditioning them;
   (b) references to supplying goods by a sale of articles as scrap (that is to say, for the value of materials included in the articles rather than for the value of the articles themselves).

(8) Where any goods have at any time been supplied by being hired out or lent to any person, neither a continuation or renewal of the hire or loan (whether on the same or different terms) nor any transaction for the transfer after that time of any interest in the goods to the person to whom they were hired or lent shall be treated for the purposes of this Act as a further supply of the goods to that person.

(9) A ship, aircraft or motor vehicle shall not be treated for the purposes of this Act as supplied to

any person by reason only that services consisting in the carriage of goods or passengers in that ship, aircraft or vehicle, or in its use for any other purpose, are provided to that person in pursuance of an agreement relating to the use of the ship, aircraft or vehicle for a particular period or for particular voyages, flights or journeys.

Amendments (Textual)

F17. Words in s. 46. (1)(d) repealed (E.W.S.) (6.4.2005) by The Regulatory Reform (Trading Stamps) Order 2005 (S.I. 2005/871), art. 6, Sch. and said words in s. 46. (1)(d) repealed (N.I.) (15.11.2005) by The Law Reform (Misccellaneous Provisions) (Northern Ireland) Order 2005 (S.I. 2005/1452) (N.I. 7), art. 24, Sch. 2; S.R. 2005/494, art. 2. (d)

F18. Words in s. 46. (4) repealed (26.5.2008) by The Consumer Protection from Unfair Trading Regulations 2008 (S.I. 2008/1277), reg. 30. (3), Sch. 4 Pt. 1 (with reg. 28. (2)(3), Sch. 3 para. 6)

F19. Words in s. 46. (7) substituted (26.5.2008) by The Consumer Protection from Unfair Trading Regulations 2008 (S.I. 2008/1277), reg. 30. (1), Sch. 2 para. 36 (with reg. 28. (2)(3))

Modifications etc. (not altering text)

C36. S. 46 applied by Wireless Telegraphy Act 1949 (c. 54, SIF 96), s. 1. C(5) as inserted by Broadcasting Act 1990 (c. 42, SIF 96), s. 170

S. 46 applied (18.9.2003 for specified purposes and 29.12.2003 for further specified purposes) by Marine Broadcasting (Offences) Act 1967 (c. 41), ss. 4, 5 (as inserted (12.12.2003) by Communications Act 2003 (c.21), ss. 408. (6)(b), 411, Sch. 17; S.I. 2003/1900, art. 2. (2), Sch. 2) (with arts. 3-6); (as amended by S.I. 2003/3142, arts. 2-4 (with arts. 5-11)

C37. S. 46 extended by Broadcasting Act 1990 (c. 42, SIF 96), s. 178. (7)

C38. S. 46. (1) applied (with modifications) (17.8.2015) by The Pyrotechnic Articles (Safety) Regulations 2015 (S.I. 2015/1553), reg. 1, Sch. 7 paras. 1. (o), 2

C39. S. 46. (1) applied (with modifications) (8.12.2016) by The Pressure Equipment (Safety) Regulations 2016 (S.I. 2016/1105), reg. 1, Sch. 7 paras. 1. (o), 2 (with reg. 88)

C40. S. 46. (1) applied (with modifications) (8.12.2016) by The Lifts Regulations 2016 (S.I. 2016/1093), reg. 1, Sch. 7 paras. 1. (n), 2 (with regs. 3-5)

C41. S. 46. (1) applied (with modifications) (8.12.2016) by The Electromagnetic Compatibility Regulations 2016 (S.I. 2016/1091), reg. 1, Sch. 7 paras. 1, 2 (with regs. 74, 75. (5))

C42. S. 46. (1) applied (with modifications) (8.12.2016) by The Simple Pressure Vessels (Safety) Regulations 2016 (S.I. 2016/1092), reg. 1, Sch. 5 paras. 1. (o), 2 (with reg. 3)

C43. S. 46. (1) applied (with modifications) (8.12.2016) by The Electrical Equipment (Safety) Regulations 2016 (S.I. 2016/1101), reg. 1, Sch. 3 paras. 1, 2 (with reg. 3)

C44. S. 46. (1) applied (with modifications) (3.8.2017) by The Recreational Craft Regulations 2017 (S.I. 2017/737), reg. 1, Sch. 13 paras. 1. (p), 2 (with reg. 89)

C45. S. 46. (1) applied (with modifications) (26.12.2017) by The Radio Equipment Regulations 2017 (S.I. 2017/1206), reg. 1, Sch. 10 paras. 1, 2 (with regs. 3-5, 77)

47 Savings for certain privileges.

(1) Nothing in this Act shall be taken as requiring any person to produce any records if he would be entitled to refuse to produce those records in any proceedings in any court on the grounds that they are the subject of legal professional privilege or, in Scotland, that they contain a confidential communication made by or to an advocate or solicitor in that capacity, or as authorising any person to take possession of any records which are in the possession of a person who would be so entitled.

(2) Nothing in this Act shall be construed as requiring a person to answer any question or give any information if to do so would incriminate that person or that person's spouse [F20or civil partner] .

Amendments (Textual)

F20. Words in s. 47. (2) inserted (5.12.2005) by Civil Partnership Act 2004 (c. 33), ss. 261. (1), 263, Sch. 27 para. 126; S.I. 2005/3175, art. 2. (2) (subject to art. 2. (3)-(5))

Modifications etc. (not altering text)

C46. S. 47 applied (with modifications) (1.1.1993) by S.I. 1992/3073, reg. 28, Sch. 6 para. 3. (c)
S. 47 applied (with modifications) (1.7.1997) by S.I. 1997/831, reg. 19. (1)-(4), Sch. 15 para. 2. (b) (with Sch. 15 para. 7)
S. 47 applied (with modifications) (31.5.1998) by S.I. 1998/1165, reg. 13. (2)(a) (which said S.I. was revoked (25.8.2003) by S.I. 2003/1941, reg. 1. (2)) S. 47 applied (with modifications) (26.4.1999) by S.I. 1999/1053, reg. 16. (3)(a)
S. 47 applied (with modifications) (29.11.1999) by S.I. 1999/2001, reg. 24, Sch. 8 para. 2. (c)
S. 47 applied (with modifications) (8.4.2000) by S.I. 2000/730, reg. 18. (1), Sch. 9 para. 1. (2)
S. 47 applied (with modifications) (15.5.2002) by S.I. 2002/1144, regs. 2. (2), 16. (1)-(3), Sch. 10 paras. 1, 3
S. 47 applied (with modifications) (25.8.2003) by S.I. 2003/1941, reg. 8, Sch. IV para. 2. (a)
S. 47 applied (E.W.S) (28.11.2003 for certain purposes, 15.7.2004 for certain further purposes and otherwise prosp.) by Fireworks Act 2003 (c. 22), ss. 13, 18 (with s. 2. (8)); S.I. 2003/3084, art. 2, Sch.; S.I. 2004/1831, art. 2, Sch.
C47. S. 47 applied (with modifications) (1.10.2015) by The Packaging (Essential Requirements) Regulations 2015 (S.I. 2015/1640), reg. 1, Sch. 4 para. 1. (1)(a) (with reg. 3. (5))

48 Minor and consequential amendments and repeals.

(1) The enactments mentioned in Schedule 4 to this Act shall have effect subject to the amendments specified in that Schedule (being minor amendments and amendments consequential on the provisions of this Act).
(2) The following Acts shall cease to have effect, that is to say—
 (a) the M8. Trade Descriptions Act 1972; and
 (b) the M9. Fabrics (Misdescription) Act 1913.
(3) The enactments mentioned in Schedule 5 to this Act are hereby repealed to the extent specified in the third column of that Schedule.
Marginal Citations
M81972 c. 34.
M91913 c. 17.

49 Northern Ireland.

(1) This Act shall extend to Northern Ireland with the exception of—
 (a) the provisions of [F21. Part 1];
 (b) any provision amending or repealing an enactment which does not so extend; and
 (c) any other provision so far as it has effect for the purposes of, or in relation to, a provision falling within paragraph (a) or (b) above.
F22. (2). . . . .
(3) An Order in Council under paragraph 1. (1)(b) of Schedule 1 to the M10. Northern Ireland Act 1974 (exercise of legislative functions for Northern Ireland) which states that it is made only for purposes corresponding to any of the provisions of this Act mentioned in subsection (1)(a) to (c) above—
 (a) shall not be subject to paragraph 1. (4) and (5) of that Schedule (affirmative resolution procedure and procedure in cases of urgency); but
 (b) shall be subject to annulment in pursuance of a resolution of either House of Parliament.
Amendments (Textual)
F21. Words in s. 49. (1)(a) substituted (26.5.2008) by The Consumer Protection from Unfair Trading Regulations 2008 (S.I. 2008/1277), reg. 30. (1), Sch. 2 para. 37 (with reg. 28. (2)(3))
F22. S. 49. (2) repealed (2.12.1999) by 1998 c. 47, s. 100. (2), Sch. 15 (with s. 95); S.I. 1999/3209, art. 2, Sch.
Marginal Citations

M101974 c. 28.

50 Short title: commencement and transitional provision.

(1) This Act may be cited as the Consumer Protection Act 1987.
(2) This Act shall come into force on such day as the Secretary of State may by order made by statutory instrument appoint, and different days may be so appointed for different provisions or for different purposes.
(3) The Secretary of State shall not make an order under subsection (2) above bringing into force the repeal of the M11. Trade Descriptions Act 1972, a repeal of any provision of that Act or a repeal of that Act or of any provision of it for any purposes, unless a draft of the order has been laid before, and approved by a resolution of, each House of Parliament.
(4) An order under subsection (2) above bringing a provision into force may contain such transitional provision in connection with the coming into force of that provision as the Secretary of State considers appropriate.
(5) Without prejudice to the generality of the power conferred by subsection (4) above, the Secretary of State may by order provide for any regulations made under the M12. Consumer Protection Act 1961 or the M13. Consumer Protection Act (Northern Ireland) 1965 to have effect as if made under section 11 above and for any such regulations to have effect with such modifications as he considers appropriate for that purpose.
(6) The power of the Secretary of State by order to make such provision as is mentioned in subsection (5) above, shall, in so far as it is not exercised by an order under subsection (2) above, be exercisable by statutory instrument subject to annulment in pursuance of a resolution of either House of Parliament.
(7) Nothing in this Act or in any order under subsection (2) above shall make any person liable by virtue of Part I of this Act for any damage caused wholly or partly by a defect in a product which was supplied to any person by its producer before the coming into force of Part I of this Act.
(8) Expressions used in subsection (7) above and in Part I of this Act have the same meanings in that subsection as in that Part.
Modifications etc. (not altering text)
C48. S. 50. (2): Power of appointment conferred by s. 50. (2) fully exercised: S.I. 1987/1680, 1988/2041, 2076
Marginal Citations
M111972 c. 34.
M121961 c. 40.
M131965 c. 14 (N. I.).

Amendments of Part I of the Health and Safety at Work etc. Act 1974.

36 Amendments of Part I of the Health and Safety at Work etc. Act 1974.

Part I of the M1. Health and Safety at Work etc. Act 1974 (which includes provision with respect to the safety of certain articles and substances) shall have effect with the amendments specified in Schedule 3 to this Act; and, accordingly, the general purposes of that Part of that Act shall include the purpose of protecting persons from the risks protection from which would not be afforded by virtue of that Part but for those amendments.
Marginal Citations

M11974 c. 37.

Schedules

Schedule 1. Limitation of Actions under Part I

Section 6.

Part I England and Wales

1. After section 11 of the M1. Limitation Act 1980 (actions in respect of personal injuries) there shall be inserted the following section—

"11. A Actions in respect of defective products.

(1) This section shall apply to an action for damages by virtue of any provision of Part I of the Consumer Protection Act 1987.
(2) None of the time limits given in the preceding provisions of this Act shall apply to an action to which this section applies.
(3) An action to which this section applies shall not be brought after the expiration of the period of ten years from the relevant time, within the meaning of section 4 of the said Act of 1987; and this subsection shall operate to extinguish a right of action and shall do so whether or not that right of action had accrued, or time under the following provisions of this Act had begun to run, at the end of the said period of ten years.
(4) Subject to subsection (5) below, an action to which this section applies in which the damages claimed by the plaintiff consist of or include damages in respect of personal injuries to the plaintiff or any other person or loss of or damage to any property, shall not be brought after the expiration of the period of three years from whichever is the later of—
    (a) the date on which the cause of action accrued; and
    (b) the date of knowledge of the injured person or, in the case of loss of or damage to property, the date of knowledge of the plaintiff or (if earlier) of any person in whom his cause of action was previously vested.
(5) If in a case where the damages claimed by the plaintiff consist of or include damages in respect of personal injuries to the plaintiff or any other person the injured person died before the expiration of the period mentioned in subsection (4) above, that subsection shall have effect as respects the cause of action surviving for the benefit of his estate by virtue of section 1 of the Law Reform (Miscellaneous Provisions) Act 1934 as if for the reference to that period there were substituted a reference to the period of three years from whichever is the later of—
    (a) the date of death; and
    (b) the date of the personal representative's knowledge.
(6) For the purposes of this section "personal representative" includes any person who is or has been a personal representative of the deceased, including an executor who has not proved the will (whether or not he has renounced probate) but not anyone appointed only as a special personal representative in relation to settled land; and regard shall be had to any knowledge acquired by any such person while a personal representative or previously.
(7) If there is more than one personal representative and their dates of knowledge are different, subsection (5)(b) above shall be read as referring to the earliest of those dates.
(8) Expressions used in this section or section 14 of this Act and in Part I of the Consumer

Protection Act 1987 have the same meanings in this section or that section as in that Part; and section 1. (1) of that Act (Part I to be construed as enacted for the purpose of complying with the product liability Directive) shall apply for the purpose of construing this section and the following provisions of this Act so far as they relate to an action by virtue of any provision of that Part as it applies for the purpose of construing that Part."

Marginal Citations
M11980 c. 58.

2. In section 12. (1) of the said Act of 1980 (actions under the M2. Fatal Accidents Act 1976), after the words "section 11" there shall be inserted the words " "or 11. A ".

Marginal Citations
M21976 c. 30.

3. In section 14 of the said Act of 1980 (definition of date of knowledge), in subsection (1), at the beginning there shall be inserted the words " "Subject to subsection (1. A) below, " and after that subsection there shall be inserted the following subsection—

"(1. A)In section 11. A of this Act and in section 12 of this Act so far as that section applies to an action by virtue of section 6. (1)(a) of the Consumer Protection Act 1987 (death caused by defective product) references to a person's date of knowledge are references to the date on which he first had knowledge of the following facts—

(a) such facts about the damage caused by the defect as would lead a reasonable person who had suffered such damage to consider it sufficiently serious to justify his instituting proceedings for damages against a defendant who did not dispute liability and was able to satisfy a judgment; and

(b) that the damage was wholly or partly attributable to the facts and circumstances alleged to constitute the defect; and

(c) the identity of the defendant;

but, in determining the date on which a person first had such knowledge there shall be disregarded both the extent (if any) of that person's knowledge on any date of whether particular facts or circumstances would or would not, as a matter of law, constitute a defect and, in a case relating to loss of or damage to property, any knowledge which that person had on a date on which he had no right of action by virtue of Part I of that Act in respect of the loss or damage."

4. In section 28 of the said Act of 1980 (extension of limitation period in case of disability), after subsection (6) there shall be inserted the following subsection—

"(7)If the action is one to which section 11. A of this Act applies or one by virtue of section 6. (1)(a) of the Consumer Protection Act 1987 (death caused by defective product), subsection (1) above—

(a) shall not apply to the time limit prescribed by subsection (3) of the said section 11. A or to that time limit as applied by virtue of section 12. (1) of this Act; and

(b) in relation to any other time limit prescribed by this Act shall have effect as if for the words "six years" there were substituted the words " "three years "."

5. In section 32 of the said Act of 1980 (postponement of limitation period in case of fraud, concealment or mistake)—

(a) in subsection (1), for the words "subsection (3)" there shall be substituted the words " "subsections (3) and (4. A) "; and

(b) after subsection (4) there shall be inserted the following subsection—

"(4. A)Subsection (1) above shall not apply in relation to the time limit prescribed by section 11. A(3) of this Act or in relation to that time limit as applied by virtue of section 12. (1) of this Act."

6. In section 33 of the said Act of 1980 (discretionary exclusion of time limit)—

(a) in subsection (1), after the words "section 11" there shall be inserted the words " "or 11. A ";

(b) after the said subsection (1) there shall be inserted the following subsection—

"(1. A)The court shall not under this section disapply—

(a) subsection (3) of section 11. A; or

(b) where the damages claimed by the plaintiff are confined to damages for loss of or damage to any property, any other provision in its application to an action by virtue of Part I of the Consumer Protection Act 1987.";

(c) in subsections (2) and (4), after the words "section 11" there shall be inserted the words " "or subsection (4) of section 11. A ";

(d) in subsection (3)(b), after the words "section 11" there shall be inserted the words " ", by section 11. A "; and

(e) in subsection (8), after the words "section 11" there shall be inserted the words " "or 11. A ".

Part II Scotland

7. The M3. Prescription and Limitation (Scotland) Act 1973 shall be amended as follows.
Marginal Citations
M31973 c .52.

8. In section 7. (2), after the words "not being an obligation" there shall be inserted the words " "to which section 22. A of this Act applies or an obligation ".

9. In Part II, before section 17, there shall be inserted the following section—

"16. A Part II not to extend to product liability.

—This Part of this Act does not apply to any action to which section 22. B or 22. C of this Act applies."

10. After section 22, there shall be inserted the following new Part—

"Part IIA Prescription of Obligations and Limitation of Actions under Part I of the Consumer Protection Act 1987

Prescription of Obligations

22. A Ten years' prescription of obligations.

(1) An obligation arising from liability under section 2 of the 1987 Act (to make reparation for damage caused wholly or partly by a defect in a product) shall be extinguished if a period of 10 years has expired from the relevant time, unless a relevant claim was made within that period and has not been finally disposed of, and no such obligation shall come into existence after the expiration of the said period.

(2) If, at the expiration of the period of 10 years mentioned in subsection (1) above, a relevant claim has been made but has not been finally disposed of, the obligation to which the claim relates shall be extinguished when the claim is finally disposed of.

(3) In this section a claim is finally disposed of when—

(a) a decision disposing of the claim has been made against which no appeal is competent;

(b) an appeal against such a decision is competent with leave, and the time limit for leave has expired and no application has been made or leave has been refused;

(c) leave to appeal against such a decision is granted or is not required, and no appeal is made within the time limit for appeal; or

(d) the claim is abandoned;

"relevant claim" in relation to an obligation means a claim made by or on behalf of the creditor for implement or part implement of the obligation, being a claim made—

(a) in appropriate proceedings within the meaning of section 4. (2) of this Act; or

(b) by the presentation of, or the concurring in, a petition for sequestration or by the submission of a claim under section 22 or 48 of the Bankruptcy (Scotland) Act 1985; or

(c) by the presentation of, or the concurring in, a petition for the winding up of a company or by the submission of a claim in a liquidation in accordance with the rules made under section 411 of the Insolvency Act 1986;

"relevant time" has the meaning given in section 4. (2) of the 1987 Act.

(4) Where a relevant claim is made in an arbitration, and the nature of the claim has been stated in

a preliminary notice (within the meaning of section 4. (4) of this Act) relating to that arbitration, the date when the notice is served shall be taken for those purposes to be the date of the making of the claim.

Limitation of actions

22. B 3 year limitation of actions.

(1) This section shall apply to an action to enforce an obligation arising from liability under section 2 of the 1987 Act (to make reparation for damage caused wholly or partly by a defect in a product), except where section 22. C of this Act applies.

(2) Subject to subsection (4) below, an action to which this section applies shall not be competent unless it is commenced within the period of 3 years after the earliest date on which the person seeking to bring (or a person who could at an earlier date have brought) the action was aware, or on which, in the opinion of the court, it was reasonably practicable for him in all the circumstances to become aware, of all the facts mentioned in subsection (3) below.

(3) The facts referred to in subsection (2) above are—

   (a) that there was a defect in a product;

   (b) that the damage was caused or partly caused by the defect;

   (c) that the damage was sufficiently serious to justify the pursuer (or other person referred to in subsection (2) above) in bringing an action to which this section applies on the assumption that the defender did not dispute liability and was able to satisfy a decree;

   (d) that the defender was a person liable for the damage under the said section 2.

(4) In the computation of the period of 3 years mentioned in subsection (2) above, there shall be disregarded any period during which the person seeking to bring the action was under legal disability by reason of nonage or unsoundness of mind.

(5) The facts mentioned in subsection (3) above do not include knowledge of whether particular facts and circumstances would or would not, as a matter of law, result in liability for damage under the said section 2.

(6) Where a person would be entitled, but for this section, to bring an action for reparation other than one in which the damages claimed are confined to damages for loss of or damage to property, the court may, if it seems to it equitable to do so, allow him to bring the action notwithstanding this section.

22. C Actions under the 1987 Act where death has resulted from personal injuries.

(1) This section shall apply to an action to enforce an obligation arising from liability under section 2 of the 1987 Act (to make reparation for damage caused wholly or partly by a defect in a product) where a person has died from personal injuries and the damages claimed include damages for those personal injuries or that death.

(2) Subject to subsection (4) below, an action to which this section applies shall not be competent unless it is commenced within the period of 3 years after the later of—

   (a) the date of death of the injured person;

   (b) the earliest date on which the person seeking to make (or a person who could at an earlier date have made) the claim was aware, or on which, in the opinion of the court, it was reasonably practicable for him in all the circumstances to become aware—

(i) that there was a defect in the product;

(ii) that the injuries of the deceased were caused (or partly caused) by the defect; and

(iii) that the defender was a person liable for the damage under the said section 2.

(3) Where the person seeking to make the claim is a relative of the deceased, there shall be disregarded in the computation of the period mentioned in subsection (2) above any period during which that relative was under legal disability by reason of nonage or unsoundness of mind.

(4) Where an action to which section 22. B of this Act applies has not been brought within the period mentioned in subsection (2) of that section and the person subsequently dies in consequence of his injuries, an action to which this section applies shall not be competent in respect of those injuries or that death.

(5) Where a person would be entitled, but for this section, to bring an action for reparation other than one in which the damages claimed are confined to damages for loss of or damage to property,

the court may, if it seems to it equitable to do so, allow him to bring the action notwithstanding this section.

(6) In this section "relative" has the same meaning as in the Damages (Scotland) Act 1976.

(7) For the purposes of subsection (2)(b) above there shall be disregarded knowledge of whether particular facts and circumstances would or would not, as a matter of law, result in liability for damage under the said section 2.

Supplementary

22. D Interpretation of this Part.

(1) Expressions used in this Part and in Part I of the 1987 Act shall have the same meanings in this Part as in the said Part I.

(2) For the purposes of section 1. (1) of the 1987 Act, this Part shall have effect and be construed as if it were contained in Part I of that Act.

(3) In this Part, "the 1987 Act" means the Consumer Protection Act 1987."

11. Section 23 shall cease to have effect, but for the avoidance of doubt it is declared that the amendments in Part II of Schedule 4 shall continue to have effect.

12. In paragraph 2 of Schedule 1, after sub-paragraph (gg) there shall be inserted the following sub-paragraph—

"(ggg)to any obligation arising from liability under section 2 of the Consumer Protection Act 1987 (to make reparation for damage caused wholly or partly by a defect in a product);".

Schedule 2. Prohibition Notices and Notices to Warn

Section 13.

Modifications etc. (not altering text)

C1. Sch. 2 applied (with modifications) (7.6.2000) by S.I. 2000/1315, reg. 18. (6)

C2. Sch. 2 applied (with modifications) (17.8.2015) by The Pyrotechnic Articles (Safety) Regulations 2015 (S.I. 2015/1553), reg. 1, Sch. 7 paras. 1. (p), 2

C3. Sch. 2 applied (with modifications) (8.12.2016) by The Electrical Equipment (Safety) Regulations 2016 (S.I. 2016/1101), reg. 1, Sch. 3 paras. 1, 2 (with reg. 3)

C4. Sch. 2 applied (with modifications) (8.12.2016) by The Simple Pressure Vessels (Safety) Regulations 2016 (S.I. 2016/1092), reg. 1, Sch. 5 paras. 1. (p), 2 (with reg. 3)

C5. Sch. 2 applied (with modifications) (8.12.2016) by The Pressure Equipment (Safety) Regulations 2016 (S.I. 2016/1105), reg. 1, Sch. 7 paras. 1. (p), 2 (with reg. 88)

C6. Sch. 2 applied (with modifications) (8.12.2016) by The Electromagnetic Compatibility Regulations 2016 (S.I. 2016/1091), reg. 1, Sch. 7 paras. 1, 2 (with regs. 74, 75. (5))

C7. Sch. 2 applied (with modifications) (8.12.2016) by The Lifts Regulations 2016 (S.I. 2016/1093), reg. 1, Sch. 7 paras. 1. (o), 2 (with regs. 3-5)

C8. Sch. 2 applied (with modifications) (3.8.2017) by The Recreational Craft Regulations 2017 (S.I. 2017/737), reg. 1, Sch. 13 paras. 1. (q), 2 (with reg. 89)

C9. Sch. 2 applied (with modifications) (26.12.2017) by The Radio Equipment Regulations 2017 (S.I. 2017/1206), reg. 1, Sch. 10 paras. 1, 2 (with regs. 3-5, 77)

Part I Prohibition Notices

1. A prohibition notice in respect of any goods shall—
(a) state that the Secretary of State considers that the goods are unsafe;
(b) set out the reasons why the Secretary of State considers that the goods are unsafe;
(c) specify the day on which the notice is to come into force; and
(d) state that the trader may at any time make representations in writing to the Secretary of State

for the purpose of establishing that the goods are safe.

2. (1) If representations in writing about a prohibition notice are made by the trader to the Secretary of State, it shall be the duty of the Secretary of State to consider whether to revoke the notice and—

(a) if he decides to revoke it, to do so;

(b) in any other case, to appoint a person to consider those representations, any further representations made (whether in writing or orally) by the trader about the notice and the statements of any witnesses examined under this Part of this Schedule.

(2) Where the Secretary of State has appointed a person to consider representations about a prohibition notice, he shall serve a notification on the trader which—

(a) states that the trader may make oral representations to the appointed person for the purpose of establishing that the goods to which the notice relates are safe; and

(b) specifies the place and time at which the oral representations may be made.

(3) The time specified in a notification served under sub-paragraph (2) above shall not be before the end of the period of twenty-one days beginning with the day on which the notification is served, unless the trader otherwise agrees.

(4) A person on whom a notification has been served under sub-paragraph (2) above or his representative may, at the place and time specified in the notification—

(a) make oral representations to the appointed person for the purpose of establishing that the goods in question are safe; and

(b) call and examine witnesses in connection with the representations.

3. (1) Where representations in writing about a prohibition notice are made by the trader to the Secretary of State at any time after a person has been appointed to consider representations about that notice, then, whether or not the appointed person has made a report to the Secretary of State, the following provisions of this paragraph shall apply instead of paragraph 2 above.

(2) The Secretary of State shall, before the end of the period of one month beginning with the day on which he receives the representations, serve a notification on the trader which states—

(a) that the Secretary of State has decided to revoke the notice, has decided to vary it or, as the case may be, has decided neither to revoke nor to vary it; or

(b) that, a person having been appointed to consider representations about the notice, the trader may, at a place and time specified in the notification, make oral representations to the appointed person for the purpose of establishing that the goods to which the notice relates are safe.

(3) The time specified in a notification served for the purposes of sub-paragraph (2)(b) above shall not be before the end of the period of twenty-one days beginning with the day on which the notification is served, unless the trader otherwise agrees or the time is the time already specified for the purposes of paragraph 2. (2)(b) above.

(4) A person on whom a notification has been served for the purposes of sub-paragraph (2)(b) above or his representative may, at the place and time specified in the notification—

(a) make oral representations to the appointed person for the purpose of establishing that the goods in question are safe; and

(b) call and examine witnesses in connection with the representations.

4. (1) Where a person is appointed to consider representations about a prohibition notice, it shall be his duty to consider—

(a) any written representations made by the trader about the notice, other than those in respect of which a notification is served under paragraph 3. (2)(a) above;

(b) any oral representations made under paragraph 2. (4) or 3. (4) above; and

(c) any statements made by witnesses in connection with the oral representations,

and, after considering any matters under this paragraph, to make a report (including recommendations) to the Secretary of State about the matters considered by him and the notice.

(2) It shall be the duty of the Secretary of State to consider any report made to him under sub-paragraph (1) above and, after considering the report, to inform the trader of his decision with respect to the prohibition notice to which the report relates.

5. (1) The Secretary of State may revoke or vary a prohibition notice by serving on the trader a

notification stating that the notice is revoked or, as the case may be, is varied as specified in the notification.
(2) The Secretary of State shall not vary a prohibition notice so as to make the effect of the notice more restrictive for the trader.
(3) Without prejudice to the power conferred by section 13. (2) of this Act, the service of a notification under sub-paragraph (1) above shall be sufficient to satisfy the requirement of paragraph 4. (2) above that the trader shall be informed of the Secretary of State's decision.

Part II Notices to Warn

6. (1)If the Secretary of State proposes to serve a notice to warn on any person in respect of any goods, the Secretary of State, before he serves the notice, shall serve on that person a notification which—
(a) contains a draft of the proposed notice;
(b) states that the Secretary of State proposes to serve a notice in the form of the draft on that person;
(c) states that the Secretary of State considers that the goods described in the draft are unsafe;
(d) sets out the reasons why the Secretary of State considers that those goods are unsafe; and
(e) states that that person may make representations to the Secretary of State for the purpose of establishing that the goods are safe if, before the end of the period of fourteen days beginning with the day on which the notification is served, he informs the Secretary of State—
(i) of his intention to make representations; and
(ii) whether the representations will be made only in writing or both in writing and orally.
(2) Where the Secretary of State has served a notification containing a draft of a proposed notice to warn on any person, he shall not serve a notice to warn on that person in respect of the goods to which the proposed notice relates unless—
(a) the period of fourteen days beginning with the day on which the notification was served expires without the Secretary of State being informed as mentioned in sub-paragraph (1)(e) above;
(b) the period of twenty-eight days beginning with that day expires without any written representations being made by that person to the Secretary of State about the proposed notice; or
(c) the Secretary of State has considered a report about the proposed notice by a person appointed under paragraph 7. (1) below.
7. (1)Where a person on whom a notification containing a draft of a proposed notice to warn has been served—
(a) informs the Secretary of State as mentioned in paragraph 6 (1)(e) above before the end of the period of fourteen days beginning with the day on which the notification was served; and
(b) makes written representations to the Secretary of State about the proposed notice before the end of the period of twenty-eight days beginning with that day,
the Secretary of State shall appoint a person to consider those representations, any further representations made by that person about the draft notice and the statements of any witnesses examined under this Part of this Schedule.
(2) Where—
(a) the Secretary of State has appointed a person to consider representations about a proposed notice to warn; and
(b) the person whose representations are to be considered has informed the Secretary of State for the purposes of paragraph 6. (1)(e) above that the representations he intends to make will include oral representations,
the Secretary of State shall inform the person intending to make the representations of the place and time at which oral representations may be made to the appointed person.
(3) Where a person on whom a notification containing a draft of a proposed notice to warn has been served is informed of a time for the purposes of sub-paragraph (2) above, that time shall not be—

(a) before the end of the period of twenty-eight days beginning with the day on which the notification was served; or
(b) before the end of the period of seven days beginning with the day on which that person is informed of the time.
(4) A person who has been informed of a place and time for the purposes of sub-paragraph (2) above or his representative may, at that place and time—
(a) make oral representations to the appointed person for the purpose of establishing that the goods to which the proposed notice relates are safe; and
(b) call and examine witnesses in connection with the representations.
8. (1)Where a person is appointed to consider representations about a proposed notice to warn, it shall be his duty to consider—
(a) any written representations made by the person on whom it is proposed to serve the notice; and
(b) in a case where a place and time has been appointed under paragraph 7. (2) above for oral representations to be made by that person or his representative, any representations so made and any statements made by witnesses in connection with those representations,
and, after considering those matters, to make a report (including recommendations) to the Secretary of State about the matters considered by him and the proposal to serve the notice.
(2) It shall be the duty of the Secretary of State to consider any report made to him under sub-paragraph (1) above and, after considering the report, to inform the person on whom it was proposed that a notice to warn should be served of his decision with respect to the proposal.
(3) If at any time after serving a notification on a person under paragraph 6 above the Secretary of State decides not to serve on that person either the proposed notice to warn or that notice with modifications, the Secretary of State shall inform that person of the decision; and nothing done for the purposes of any of the preceding provisions of this Part of this Schedule before that person was so informed shall—
(a) entitle the Secretary of State subsequently to serve the proposed notice or that notice with modifications; or
(b) require the Secretary of State, or any person appointed to consider representations about the proposed notice, subsequently to do anything in respect of, or in consequence of, any such representations.
(4) Where a notification containing a draft of a proposed notice to warn is served on a person in respect of any goods, a notice to warn served on him in consequence of a decision made under sub-paragraph (2) above shall either be in the form of the draft or shall be less onerous than the draft.
9. The Secretary of State may revoke a notice to warn by serving on the person on whom the notice was served a notification stating that the notice is revoked.

Part III General

10. (1)Where in a notification served on any person under this Schedule the Secretary of State has appointed a time for the making of oral representations or the examination of witnesses, he may, by giving that person such notification as the Secretary of State considers appropriate, change that time to a later time or appoint further times at which further representations may be made or the examination of witnesses may be continued; and paragraphs 2. (4), 3. (4) and 7. (4) above shall have effect accordingly.
(2) For the purposes of this Schedule the Secretary of State may appoint a person (instead of the appointed person) to consider any representations or statements, if the person originally appointed, or last appointed under this sub-paragraph, to consider those representations or statements has died or appears to the Secretary of State to be otherwise unable to act.
11. In this Schedule—
"the appointed person" in relation to a prohibition notice or a proposal to serve a notice to warn, means the person for the time being appointed under this Schedule to consider representations

about the notice or, as the case may be, about the proposed notice;

"notification" means a notification in writing;

"trader", in relation to a prohibition notice, means the person on whom the notice is or was served.

Schedule 3. Amendments of Part I of the Health and Safety at Work etc. Act 1974

Section 36.

1. (1)Section 6 (general duties of manufacturers etc. as regard articles and substances for use at work) shall be amended as follows.

(2) For subsection (1) (general duties of designers, manufacturers, importers and suppliers of articles for use at work) there shall be substituted the following subsections—

"(1)It shall be the duty of any person who designs, manufactures, imports or supplies any article for use at work or any article of fairground equipment—

  (a) to ensure, so far as is reasonably practicable, that the article is so designed and constructed that it will be safe and without risks to health at all times when it is being set, used, cleaned or maintained by a person at work;

  (b) to carry out or arrange for the carrying out of such testing and examination as may be necessary for the performance of the duty imposed on him by the preceding paragraph;

  (c) to take such steps as are necessary to secure that persons supplied by that person with the article are provided with adequate information about the use for which the article is designed or has been tested and about any conditions necessary to ensure that it will be safe and without risks to health at all such times as are mentioned in paragraph (a) above and when it is being dismantled or disposed of; and

  (d) to take such steps as are necessary to secure, so far as is reasonably practicable, that persons so supplied are provided with all such revisions of information provided to them by virtue of the preceding paragraph as are necessary by reason of its becoming known that anything gives rise to a serious risk to health or safety.

(1. A)It shall be the duty of any person who designs, manufactures, imports or supplies any article of fairground equipment—

  (a) to ensure, so far as is reasonably practicable, that the article is so designed and constructed that it will be safe and without risks to health at all times when it is being used for or in connection with the entertainment of members of the public;

  (b) to carry out or arrange for the carrying out of such testing and examination as may be necessary for the performance of the duty imposed on him by the preceding paragraph;

  (c) to take such steps as are necessary to secure that persons supplied by that person with the article are provided with adequate information about the use for which the article is designed or has been tested and about any conditions necessary to ensure that it will be safe and without risks to health at all times when it is being used for or in connection with the entertainment of members of the public; and

  (d) to take such steps as are necessary to secure, so far as is reasonably practicable, that persons so supplied are provided with all such revisions of information provided to them by virtue of the preceding paragraph as are necessary by reason of its becoming known that anything gives rise to a serious risk to health or safety."

(3) In subsection (2) (duty of person who undertakes the design or manufacture of an article for use at work to carry out research), after the word "work" there shall be inserted the words " "or of any article of fairground equipment ".

(4) In subsection (3) (duty of persons who erect or install articles for use at work)—

(a) after the words "persons at work" there shall be inserted the words " "or who erects or installs any article of fairground equipment "; and

(b) for the words from "it is" onwards there shall be substituted the words " "the article is erected or installed makes it unsafe or a risk to health at any such time as is mentioned in paragraph (a) of subsection (1) or, as the case may be, in paragraph (a) of subsection (1) or (1. A) above. "

(5) For subsection (4) (general duties of manufacturers, importers and suppliers of substances for use at work) there shall be substituted the following subsection—

"(4)It shall be the duty of any person who manufactures, imports or supplies any substance—

(a) to ensure, so far as is reasonably practicable, that the substance will be safe and without risks to health at all times when it is being used, handled, processed, stored or transported by a person at work or in premises to which section 4 above applies;

(b) to carry out or arrange for the carrying out of such testing and examination as may be necessary for the performance of the duty imposed on him by the preceding paragraph;

(c) to take such steps as are necessary to secure that persons supplied by that person with the substance are provided with adequate information about any risks to health or safety to which the inherent properties of the substance may give rise, about the results of any relevant tests which have been carried out on or in connection with the substance and about any conditions necessary to ensure that the substance will be safe and without risks to health at all such times as are mentioned in paragraph (a) above and when the substance is being disposed of; and

(d) to take such steps as are necessary to secure, so far as is reasonably practicable, that persons so supplied are provided with all such revisions of information provided to them by virtue of the preceding paragraph as are necessary by reason of its becoming known that anything gives rise to a serious risk to health or safety."

(6) In subsection (5) (duty of person who undertakes the manufacture of a substance for use at work to carry out research)—

(a) for the words "substance for use at work" there shall be substituted the word " "substance "; and

(b) at the end there shall be inserted the words " "at all such times as are mentioned in paragraph (a) of subsection (4) above ".

(7) In subsection (8) (relief from duties for persons relying on undertakings by others)—

(a) for the words "for or to another" there shall be substituted the words " "for use at work or an article of fairground equipment and does so for or to another ";

(b) for the words "when properly used" there shall be substituted the words " "at all such times as are mentioned in paragraph (a) of subsection (1) or, as the case may be, in paragraph (a) of subsection (1) or (1. A) above "; and

(c) for the words "by subsection (1)(a) above" there shall be substituted the words " "by virtue of that paragraph ".

(8) After the said subsection (8) there shall be inserted the following subsection—

"(8. A)Nothing in subsection (7) or (8) above shall relieve any person who imports any article or substance from any duty in respect of anything which—

(a) in the case of an article designed outside the United Kingdom, was done by and in the course of any trade, profession or other undertaking carried on by, or was within the control of, the person who designed the article; or

(b) in the case of an article or substance manufactured outside the United Kingdom, was done by and in the course of any trade, profession or other undertaking carried on by, or was within the control of, the person who manufactured the article or substance."

(9) In subsection (9) (definition of supplier in certain cases of supply under a hire-purchase agreement), for the words "article for use at work or substance for use at work" there shall be substituted the words " "article or substance ".

(10) For subsection (10) (meaning of "properly used") there shall be substituted the following subsection—

"(10)For the purposes of this section an absence of safety or a risk to health shall be disregarded in so far as the case in or in relation to which it would arise is shown to be one the occurrence of which could not reasonably be foreseen; and in determining whether any duty imposed by virtue of paragraph (a) of subsection (1), (1. A) or (4) above has been performed regard shall be had to any relevant information or advice which has been provided to any person by the person by whom the article has been designed, manufactured, imported or supplied or, as the case may be, by the person by whom the substance has been manufactured, imported or supplied."

2. In section 22 (prohibition notices)—

(a) in subsections (1) and (2) (notices in respect of activities which are or are about to be carried on and involve a risk of serious personal injury), for the word "about", in each place where it occurs, there shall be substituted the word " "likely ";

(b) for subsection (4) (notice to have immediate effect only if the risk is imminent) there shall be substituted the following subsection—

"(4)A direction contained in a prohibition notice in pursuance of subsection (3)(d) above shall take effect—

    (a) at the end of the period specified in the notice; or

    (b) if the notice so declares, immediately."

3. After section 25 there shall be inserted the following section—

"25. A Power of customs officer to detain articles and substances.

(1) A customs officer may, for the purpose of facilitating the exercise or performance by any enforcing authority or inspector of any of the powers or duties of the authority or inspector under any of the relevant statutory provisions, seize any imported article or imported substance and detain it for not more than two working days.

(2) Anything seized and detained under this section shall be dealt with during the period of its detention in such manner as the Commissioners of Customs and Excise may direct.

(3) In subsection (1) above the reference to two working days is a reference to a period of forty-eight hours calculated from the time when the goods in question are seized but disregarding so much of any period as falls on a Saturday or Sunday or on Chistmas Day, Good Friday or a day which is a bank holiday under the Banking and Financial Dealings Act 1971 in the part of Great Britain where the goods are seized."

4. After section 27 (power to obtain information) there shall be inserted the following section—

"27. A Information communicated by the Commissioners of Customs and Excise.

(1) If they think it appropriate to do so for the purpose of facilitating the exercise or performance by any person to whom subsection (2) below applies of any of that person's powers or duties under any of the relevant statutory provisions, the Commissioners of Customs and Excise may authorise the disclosure to that person of any information obtained for the purposes of the exercise by the Commissioners of their functions in relation to imports.

(2) This subsection applies to an enforcing authority and to an inspector.

(3) A disclosure of information made to any person under subsection (1) above shall be made in such manner as may be directed by the Commissioners of Customs and Excise and may be made through such persons acting on behalf of that person as may be so directed.

(4) Information may be disclosed to a person under subsection (1) above whether or not the disclosure of the information has been requested by or on behalf of that person."

5. In section 28 (restrictions on disclosure of information), in subsection (1)(a), after the words "furnished to any person" there shall be inserted the words " "under section 27. A above or ".

6. In section 33. (1)(h) (offence of obstructing an inspector), after the word "duties" there shall be inserted the words " "or to obstruct a customs officer in the exercise of his powers under section 25. A ".

7. In section 53. (1) (general interpretation of Part I)—

(a) after the definition of "article for use at work" there shall be inserted the following definition—
" "article of fairground equipment" means any fairground equipment or any article designed for use as a component in any such equipment;"
(b) after the definition of "credit-sale agreement" there shall be inserted the following definition—
" "customs officer" means an officer within the meaning of the Customs and Excise Management Act 1979;"
(c) before the definition of "the general purposes of this Part" there shall be inserted the following definition—
" "fairground equipment" means any fairground ride, any similar plant which is designed to be in motion for entertainment purposes with members of the public on or inside it or any plant which is designed to be used by members of the public for entertainment purposes either as a slide or for bouncing upon, and in this definition the reference to plant which is designed to be in motion with members of the public on or inside it includes a reference to swings, dodgems and other plant which is designed to be in motion wholly or partly under the control of, or to be put in motion by, a member of the public;"
(d) after the definition of "local authority" there shall be inserted the following definition—
" "micro-organism" includes any microscopic biological entity which is capable of replication;"
(e) in the definition of "substance", after the words "natural or artificial substance" there shall be inserted the words " "(including micro-organisms) ".

Schedule 4. Minor and Consequential Amendments

Section 48.

The Explosives M1. Act 1875.

Marginal Citations
M11875 c. 17.
1. In sections 31 and 80 of the Explosives Act 1875 (prohibitions on selling gunpowder to children and on use of fireworks in public places), for the words from "shall be liable" onwards there shall be substituted the words " "shall be guilty of an offence and liable on summary conviction to a fine not exceeding level 5 on the standard scale ".

The M2. Trade Descriptions Act 1968.

Marginal Citations
M21968 c. 29.
2. (1)In section 2 of the Trade Descriptions Act 1968 (meaning of trade description)—
(a) for paragraph (g) of subsection (4) (marks and descriptions applied in pursuance of the M3. Consumer Safety Act 1978) there shall be substituted the following paragraph—
   "(g)the Consumer Protection Act 1987;" and
(b) in subsection (5)(a) (descriptions prohibited under certain enactments), for the words "or the Consumer Safety Act 1978" there shall be substituted the words " "or the Consumer Protection Act 1987 ".
(2) F1. . . . .
Amendments (Textual)
F1. Sch. 4 para. 2. (2) repealed (20.6.2003) by 2002 c. 40, ss. 278. (2), 279, Sch. 26; S.I. 2003/1397, art. 2. (1), Sch. (with art. 10)

Marginal Citations
M31978 c. 38.

The M4. Fair Trading Act 1973.

Marginal Citations
M41973 c. 41.
3. F2. . . . .
Amendments (Textual)
F2. Sch. 4 para. 3 repealed (20.6.2003) by 2002 c. 40, ss. 278. (2), 279, Sch. 26; S.I. 2003/1397, art. 2. (1), Sch. (with art. 10)

The M5. Consumer Credit Act 1974.

Marginal Citations
M51974 c. 39.
4. F3. . . . .
Amendments (Textual)
F3. Sch. 4 para. 4 repealed (20.6.2003) by 2002 c. 40, ss. 278. (2), 279, Sch. 26; S.I. 2003/1397, art. 2. (1), Sch. (with art. 10)

The Torts (Interference with Goods) Act 1977.

5. In section 1 of the M6. Torts (Interference with Goods) Act 1977 (meaning of "wrongful interference"), after paragraph (d) there shall be inserted the following words—
"and references in this Act (however worded) to proceedings for wrongful interference or to a claim or right to claim for wrongful interference shall include references to proceedings by virtue of Part I of the Consumer Protection Act 1987 (product liability) in respect of any damage to goods or to an interest in goods or, as the case may be, to a claim or right to claim by virtue of that Part in respect of any such damage."
Marginal Citations
M61977 c. 32.

The M7. Estate Agents Act 1979.

Marginal Citations
M71979 c. 38.
6. In section 10. (3)(a) of the Estate Agents Act 1979 (exceptions to general restrictions on disclosure of information), after the words "or the Airports Act 1986" there shall be inserted the words " "or the Consumer Protection Act 1987. "

The M8. Competition Act 1980.

Marginal Citations
M81980 c. 21.
7. F4. . . . .
Amendments (Textual)
F4. Sch. 4 para. 7 repealed (20.6.2003) by 2002 c. 40, ss. 278. (2), 279, Sch. 26; S.I. 2003/1397, art. 2. (1), Sch. (with art. 10)

The M9. Employment Act 1982.

Marginal Citations
M9 1982 c. 46.
F58. . . . .
Amendments (Textual)
F5. Sch. 4 para. 8 repealed (16.10.1992) by Trade Union and Labour Relations (Consolidation) Act 1992 (c. 52), ss. 300. (1), 302, Sch.1

The M10. Telecommunications Act 1984.

Marginal Citations
M10 1984 c. 12.
9. (1)F6. . . . .
(2) In section 101. (3) of the said Act of 1984 (enactments specified in exceptions to general restrictions on disclosure of information), after paragraph (g) there shall be inserted the following paragraph—
　"(h)the Consumer Protection Act 1987."
Amendments (Textual)
F6. Sch. 4 para. 9. (1) repealed (8.2.2007) by Wireless Telegraphy Act 2006 (c. 36), ss. 125, 126, Sch. 9 Pt. 1

The M11. Airports Act 1986.

Marginal Citations
M11 1986 c. 31.
10. In section 74. (3) of the Airports Act 1986 (enactments specified in exceptions to general restrictions on disclosure of information), after paragraph (h) there shall be inserted the following paragraph—
　"(i)the Consumer Protection Act 1987."

The M12. Gas Act 1986.

Marginal Citations
M12 1986 c. 44.
11. In section 42 of the Gas Act 1986—
(a) in subsection (3) (restrictions on disclosure of information except for the purposes of certain enactments), at the end there shall be inserted the following paragraph—
　"(j)the Consumer Protection Act 1987.";
(b) after subsection (5) there shall be inserted the following subsection—
"(6)In relation to the Consumer Protection Act 1987 the reference in subsection (2)(b) above to a weights and measures authority shall include a reference to any person on whom functions under that Act are conferred by regulations under section 27. (2) of that Act."

The M13. Insolvency Act 1986.

Marginal Citations
M13 1986 c. 45.
12. In section 281. (5)(a) of the Insolvency Act 1986 (discharge from bankruptcy not to release bankrupt from liability in respect of personal injuries), for the word "being" there shall be substituted the words " "or to pay damages by virtue of Part I of the Consumer Protection Act

1987, being in either case ".

The M14. Motor Cycle Noise Act 1987.

Marginal Citations
M141987 c. 34.
13. For paragraphs 3 to 5 of the Schedule to the Motor Cycle Noise Act 1987 (enforcement) there shall be substituted the following paragraph—
"3. Part IV of the Consumer Protection Act 1987 (enforcement), except section 31 (power of customs officers to detain goods), shall have effect as if the provisions of this Act were safety provisions within the meaning of that Act; and in Part V of that Act (miscellaneous and supplemental), except in section 49 (Northern Ireland), references to provisions of the said Part IV shall include references to those provisions as applied by this paragraph."

Schedule 5. Repeals

Section 48.

Chapter	Short title	Extent of repeal
3 & 4 Geo. 5. c. 17.	The Fabrics (Misdescription) Act 1913.	The whole Act.
1967 c. 80.	The Criminal Justice Act 1967.	In Part I of Schedule 3, the entry relating to the Fabrics (Misdescription) Act 1913.
1967 c. 29. (N.I.).	The Fines Act (Northern Ireland) 1967.	In Part I of the Schedule, the entry relating to the Fabrics (Misdescription) Act 1913.
1968 c. 29.	The Trade Descriptions Act 1968.	Section 11.
1972 c. 34.	The Trade Descriptions Act 1972.	The whole Act.
1972 c. 70.	The Local Government Act 1972.	In Part II of Schedule 29, paragraph 18(1).
1973 c. 52.	The Prescription and Limitation (Scotland) Act 1973.	Section 23.
1973 c. 65.	The Local Government (Scotland) Act 1973.	In Part II of Schedule 27, paragraph 50.
1974 c. 37.	The Health and Safety at Work etc. Act 1974.	In section 53(1), the definition of "substance for use at work".
1976 c. 26.	The Explosives (Age of Purchase etc.) Act 1976.	In section 1, in subsection (1), the words from "and for the word" onwards and subsection (2).
1978 c. 38.	The Consumer Safety Act 1978.	The whole Act.
1980 c. 43.	The Magistrates' Courts Act 1980.	In Schedule 7, paragraphs 172 and 173.
1984 c. 12.	The Telecommunications Act 1984.	In section 101(3)(f), the word "and".
1984 c. 30.	The Food Act 1984.	In Schedule 10, paragraph 32.
1986 c. 29.	The Consumer Safety (Amendment) Act 1986.	The whole Act.
1986 c. 31.	The Airports Act 1986.	In section 74(3)(g), the word "and".
1986 c. 44.	The Gas Act 1986.	In section 42(3), paragraphs (a) and (g) and, in paragraph (h), the word "and".

Open Government Licence v3.0

Contains public sector information licensed under the Open Government Licence v3.0.
The full licence if available at the following address:
http://www.nationalarchives.gov.uk/doc/open-government-licence/version/3/

Printed in Great Britain
by Amazon